Home Buying and Financing

101

Save Thousands

Second Edition

by

Mark Kovach

ISBN: 978-0-692-18062-4

Dedication

I would like to dedicate this book to Joan, my wife and the most wonderful lady, lover, friend, companion, and soul mate a man could ever ask for in this world. Joan has been my inspiration over the years and without her constant nagging at me, in a very nice way, I would have never finished this book nor the other book that I had started years ago and just finished in 2008 that was designed to teach everyone about the inter-workings of home buying and what mortgage loans are good and which ones are bad and need to be avoided at all cost and is entitled *"Home Buying and Financing 101."* Joan has been there by my side encouraging and motivating me and she has been my best helper, and companion throughout the years I have been writing these couple of books. Also, I would like to extend a very special thank you to the two most wonderful children a man could ask for, and they are my son Lance and my daughter Sherrell. Both of my kids are grown now, but nevertheless, they have been great contributors to both of my books even though they did not realize it, because I had learned so much from them as they were growing up with Joan and me. I just want to thank Joan, Lance and Sherrell for all their contributions, and the patience they had to endure over the years while growing up with me, and to let all of you know how proud I am to have them as my family.

Introduction

Home Buying and Financing 101 was created and developed by Mark S. Kovach, and it includes excerpts from the *Professional Real-Estate Loan Officer's Course and Reference Manual*, which was also created, developed, and authored by Mr. Kovach and was taught at the Professional Loan Officer Training Center, which was located in Southern California before its closure following the refinance boom that occurred in the early 1990s.

The author is the foremost leading expert and authority in the United States concerning the negative adjustable home loan, that he states is the best home loan in the entire loan marketplace, and a loan that anyone can drive like one's own car while driving the banks crazy! Mr. Kovach maintains a Bachelor of Business Administration Degree with a major in Business Management in addition to a Masters Degree in Business Finance. The author was a licensed real-estate mortgage loan consultant who funded millions of dollars' worth of real estate throughout the United States with the majority of his loan business being conducted in Southern California. He also spent a number of years structuring, negotiating, and funding commercial loan projects in the millions and hundreds of millions of dollars for his clients.

Because of the author's extensive dealings with the real-estate finance industry, he realized a major need for a professional, instructional home loan information book that would fill a major educational gap that currently exists in the mortgage loan industry throughout the United States. This book was written to educate mortgage loan consultants, loan officers, and other lenders in the loan business in order to allow them the opportunity to gain the knowledge that is required for them to be able to assist their loan clients without recommending loan programs that would hurt their clients, put them in jeopardy, or force them into foreclosures.

Furthermore, Mr. Kovach realized the need to create equal opportunity for first-time homebuyers, as well as, the seasoned professional real-estate investors, by giving them a way to become educated and knowledgeable in understanding exactly what is involved in a real-estate transaction. Likewise, Mr. Kovach also saw a need for the general home-buying public to be able to understand the majority of the home buying categories the homebuyers will be exposed to, and have to make decisions on, when they are buying their home. Furthermore, we will also show and explain a myriad of the various loan programs that they may be offered to the homebuyers when purchasing a home, or refinancing a home loan, as well as, explaining the inner workings of various loan programs that may be offered to them by the mortgage loan industry. Therefore, and with extensive research and evaluation the author created and developed a revised second edition of *"Home Buying & Financing 101"* that includes new updates, and subjects such as the Reverse Mortgage and other information that was designed for the benefit of the general home-buying public. Having spent a combination of approximately 36 years in the real estate and loan industries Mr. Kovach continues to act in the capacity of a financial consultant and advisor to the real estate brokers, lenders, loan consultants and loan officers and a few of his long term clients. Likewise we are wishing you good fortune in your selection of your new home purchase and the loan programs that you are entitled to in all of your future real-estate investment endeavors!

Sincerely,

Mark S. Kovach, Residential/Commercial Mortgage Loan Consultant.

Contents

SECTION 1: LOAN PROCESSING

How to Get a Home Loan 1

Should We Apply To More Than One Lender?..........1

What Is Needed To Make a Home Loan Application?
....3

How Long Should It Take to Get a Home Loan? 6

Do We Have the Option to Choose a Lender?............8

Do You Recommend Contacting a Lender First to
Pre-qualify?...12

Is There Any Such Thing as a Loan Approval or Loan
Pre-approval? 13

Are There Hidden Costs in Getting a Home Loan?..16

What Are Garbage Fees? And Do They Still Exist?.18

What Are Credit Scores? And Can They Affect
Mortgage Rates? 21

SECTION 2: COST AND RATES

What Are Rates, and How Are They Determined?...30

Are There Home Loan Indicators Concerning Interest
Rates?...31

Does the Stock Market Affect Interest Rates? 36

Would It Be Better to Wait for Rates to Go Down
before We Buy a Home?..37

When Can I Lock In an Interest Rate, and Is It
Feasible? 39

How to Compare Loans and Their Costs? 40

What Are Points? 44

What Is a Prepayment Penalty, and Do We Have to
Accept It? 50

What Is Escrow, and Is It Required? 52

What Is Title Insurance, and Is It Required? 56

What Is PMI, MIP, and VA Insurance? 61

Is It a Requirement to Have Private Mortgage
Insurance (PMI)? 62

Is It a Requirement to Always Have to Pay PMI, MIP,
and VA Insurance? 62

SECTION 3: PARTS OF A LOAN AND LOAN COMPARISONS

What Is a Margin or Spread? 65

What Is a Loan Cap? 67

Start Rate vs. Margin vs. Note Rate vs. Index vs.
Payment Cap or Interest-Rate Loan Cap VS Life Cap
....72

Are Fixed Rates More Expensive Than Adjustable
Rates? 75

Are There Better Loan Programs Available with
Lower Start Rates? 85

What Is a Conversion-Option Loan? 88

What Are Negative Loans, and Are They Beneficial?
....90

What Is the Worst Home Loan on the Market? 127

Loan Broker vs. Mortgage Banker vs. Direct Lender
....135

What Is Bait-and-Switch, and Does It Apply to the
Lending Industry? 140

SECTION 4: DANGEROUS LOANS

Dangerous Mortgage Loans to Avoid 150

Dangerous Margins/Spreads 160

Dangerous Indexes to Avoid 161

Dangerous Life Caps to Avoid 167

Dangerous Start Rates to Avoid 169

The Reverse Mortgage 175

The Intelligent Smart Way to Buy a Home without
Going Broke or ever Losing your Home 182

BONUS SECTION

Preface...191

People in Banking...192

Learning to Use Your Bank 197

Standard Banking Operations 202

What Bankers Want To See....................................207

The Beginning of Credit 209

How to Expand Your Credit 213

Small Business Credit...217

Learn and Know Your Bank's Limits....................220

It Can be Worth it to Shop Around........................224

Things to Remember About Banks and Banking ...227

SECTION 1: LOAN PROCESSING

How to Get a Home Loan

Fortunately, there are many sources available for mortgage loans, and the largest being the savings-and-loan associations. Unfortunately, the majority of the S & Ls not only have unfavorable rates and margins concerning adjustable-interest-rate loans, but also lifetime caps. Mortgage brokers are, on the other hand, becoming the lenders of the future because of their ability to use and compare multiple lending sources, thereby enabling them to select the best mortgage loans for their clients. Mortgage loan brokers are direct and indirect lenders who fund your loan and then sell your loan to the investors in the secondary mortgage market. Please don't misunderstand, as the majority of the direct lenders (the savings-and-loan associations) will also sell your mortgage loan in the secondary market, and I will explain why later.

Should We Apply To More Than One Lender?

Yes! The assumption is that homebuyers will want to make sure that they are getting the lowest interest rates possible when it is time for them to close their home loan transaction. If this is the case, how do homebuyers decide which lender to use? Should homebuyers be concerned about getting the lowest interest rates possible in the current marketplace, then I suggest the homebuyers use a reputable mortgage loan broker for the following reason: Making multiple loan applications will require homebuyers to provide the same information to all of the lending institutions, and each lender will require the homebuyers to pay for a credit report and appraisal fees in advance.

Therefore, should you be one of those homebuyers who are into shopping loans with lenders, then be careful, as this could become very expensive depending on the number of applications that you submit, and at the same time, each credit report pulled could lower your overall credit score (see section on credit). However, a good mortgage loan broker will have access to many excellent banks and lending sources to shop with in order to get you the best home loans available that will require only one loan application, one credit report fee, and one appraisal fee.

Furthermore, homebuyers should know and understand, that in the event their loan is not approved, the mortgage loan broker or mortgage banker will more than likely resubmit your loan to another lending institution for approval, and usually without the homebuyers' knowledge. The benefit to the homebuyers is that a good mortgage loan broker or mortgage banker will submit, and can resubmit your loan to various lenders, and real-estate investors seeking to receive an approval for their clients' home loans without any additional cost to the homebuyers. Please note: All lenders (mortgage loan brokers, mortgage bankers, savings and loans, etc.) acquire their funds from the same financial entities in the mortgage loan marketplace. Therefore, the interest rates will not, and should not vary that much from one lender to the next.

What Is Needed To Make a Home Loan Application?

Should the homebuyers be fortunate enough to get a qualified mortgage loan consultant or loan officer (see section: Are There Home Loan Indicators Concerning Interest Rates?), they will ask for anything and everything that has to do with the homebuyers' past and current financial and credit histories. The homebuyers will need to supply current pay stubs along with their W-2 forms, and if the homebuyers are self-employed or have rental properties, they will need two previous years of tax returns, which should include complete personal, partnership, or corporate tax returns in addition to year-to-date profit-and-loss statements (prepared by a CPA). Homebuyers will be required to supply their bank statements, stock or bond certificates or statements (or copies from their stock broker's account), retirement IRAs, 401k statements, etc., along with life insurance policies if there is a face value. Furthermore, if any of the homebuyers have been divorced within the last two years, you will need your divorce decree to verify any support or other monies they may be required to pay or receive. Basically, the more information the mortgage loan Consultant or loan officer can accumulate from the homebuyers in the beginning of their home loan application, the easier it will be to expedite and secure the homebuyers' home loan.

Caution! Homebuyers *need to* and *must* understand that the mortgage loan consultant or loan officer they decide to do business with must have the mortgage loan consultant or loan officer's full and complete trust and confidence to be able to reveal *anything* and *everything* to their mortgage loan consultant or loan officer that may affect the processing of the homebuyers' home loan application. In other words, do not lie to or try to hide any information from the mortgage loan consultant or loan officer. Trust me on this one. Once the homebuyers have completed the home loan application, the mortgage loan consultants or loan officers return the loan application to be submitted and opened for processing at their respective company.

When the loan processors take over the homebuyers' loan applications, they will be making all sorts of inquiries concerning the homebuyers until they are satisfied that *all* the homebuyers' information has been checked and verified. Even though there is a wide range of so-called qualified loan processors in the mortgage loan industry, and even though these processors are subject to overlooking important items because of their lack of experience, they all maintain one common denominator—the loan underwriter, who I can personally guarantee will not overlook anything concerning the homebuyers. These underwriters are the people who make or break the potential homebuyer's ability to purchase or refinance a home loan. The homebuyers need to understand that the loan underwriters are extremely experienced and technical people who are trained to meticulously scrutinize every detail of the loan documentation. Therefore, if anything at all turns up or even looks suspicious (and it always does), the homebuyer's loan application is put on hold until any and all conditions in question have been resolved to the loan underwriter's satisfaction.

Before moving on, I need to point out to the homebuyers that the majority of all mortgage loan consultants and loan officers are licensed real-estate agents throughout the United States, and therefore, they maintain a responsibility and a fiduciary duty to assist and protect their clients' information and confidentiality at all times. To put this into its proper perspective, these mortgage loan consultants and loan officers maintain the same type of code of ethics as doctors and their clients, lawyers and their clients, etc., and should, therefore, be given as much information by the homebuyers as needed, whether it's good or bad, in order to allow the mortgage loan consultants and loan officers to get the homebuyers' home loans approved as expeditiously as possible.

As a retired loan consultant myself, I couldn't begin to tell you how many times I've had home loan applications suspended because my clients tried to hide something from me in the beginning of the loan process. Not only did this cost me a lot of time, and cause me a lot of frustration and aggravation, but it also forced the homebuyers to have their home loans extended past their due dates, and in some cases cancelled altogether simply because they thought I would not find out about some particular late payment or another piece of property they owned or some new development that occurred while the homebuyers were in the middle of the home loan application process. It never ceased to amaze me why homebuyers thought they could hide material information from their mortgage loan consultants and loan officers only to be confronted with this information late in the loan process, thereby causing delays, and further explanations in order to resolve the problems that I could have handled in the beginning, had the homebuyers been up front with me. Finally, another factor that used to amaze me was when homebuyers became vague or deceptive when it came to asking them about their finances. Give me a break! As a loan officer, I financed hundreds of millions of dollars worth of residential and commercial real estate for a lot of different people, companies, and corporations over several years, and to think that I could ever possibly remember who made what, and when and where they made it, is absolutely ludicrous, and yet for some reason or other, homebuyers are reluctant to reveal their financial information, and still expect us, as mortgage loan consultants and loan officers, to get them their new home mortgage or refinance their existing home loan. The bottom line, homebuyers, is to be honest and up front in the beginning of your mortgage loan or refinancing application with your mortgage loan consultant or loan officer, and you will be glad you did in the long run!

How Long Should It Take to Get a Home Loan?

This is a very good question. In the event the homebuyers find a qualified loan consultant or loan officer, and providing they request the necessary information and documentation (which the homebuyers provide), a mortgage loan can be processed and closed within twenty to thirty days. However, closing times may vary depending upon the loan consultant or loan officer that the homebuyers deal with, along with any complications that may arise concerning the creditability of the homebuyers. Nonetheless, and excluding government mortgage loans and any further complications, mortgage loans should not take longer than thirty to forty-five days. Therefore, it is my recommendation that during the beginning of the application for a mortgage loan, homebuyers ask lenders what their normal loan processing time is to close a home loan transaction.

Furthermore, and this is very important, ask the lender if they have an in-house underwriter. The reason for this question is that an in-house underwriter is usually familiar with most of the funding lenders and investors underwriting loan guidelines, which in turn, allows them to pre-underwrite mortgage loans according to those funding guidelines. Then it is simply a matter of the mortgage loan broker submitting the homebuyers' mortgage loan request to the appropriate lenders or investors, who then send the loan application to their underwriters for final loan approval that has already been pre-underwritten to their guidelines. At this point it just becomes a process of final review by the lenders' or investors' underwriters, who simply have to make sure that all the information and documentation is in order according to their guidelines.

Once approved by the funding underwriter, the order for the final mortgage loan documentation is made, and an appointment for signing with the homebuyers takes place within a day or so, depending on the availability of the homebuyers. Once the mortgage loan documentation has been signed by the homebuyers, the final mortgage loan funding will take place within the next three to five days, unless the mortgage loan documentation is signed on a Friday, in which case the mortgage loan will fund within three to five working weekdays. Likewise, should the loan be an owner occupied refinance or second mortgage loan the owners will maintain a three-day right of rescission that must expire before the loan can be funded. However, with a non-owner (N/O) occupant loan, the loan will not have a three-day right of rescission. Remember, mortgage loan brokers and lenders who maintain in-house underwriters can give the homebuyers a big advantage over the lenders who do not have in-house underwriters, especially, if the homebuyers have to close their mortgage loan in a very short period of time. Nevertheless, it should also be noted, that even though a mortgage loan broker or lender does not maintain in-house underwriters, they can still function in a timely manner, depending on how good their loan processors are at compiling information and documentation from the homebuyers.

Do We Have the Option to Choose a Lender?

Yes! However, even though your real-estate agent or the real-estate company may recommend a lender, be extremely careful and proceed with caution, as homebuyers may become subjected to *steering*, which is against the law according to the Department of Real Estate in the state of California and possibly in other states. Nonetheless, in the event that your real-estate agent or the real estate company recommends that you use their in-house lender, or the real-estate agent or real-estate company suggest that the homebuyers use a particular lender, be sure to question the real-estate agent's or real-estate company's broker as to why they are making their recommendation for the homebuyers to use a specific or specified lender.

In any event, homebuyers should know that not only do these real-estate companies make their monies from real-estate transactions, but they also make more money by getting the homebuyers to use their in-house lender. Furthermore, it is also important for homebuyers to realize that they have the right to select any mortgage loan consultant, loan officer, or lender that they would like to have to finance their home loan. Moreover, even if the real-estate agent or the company's broker recommends a specific or specified loan officer or lender, the homebuyers should know that they also have the right to ask the real-estate agent or company broker for recommendations of additional mortgage loan consultants, loan officers, or lenders that are not affiliated or associated with the real-estate agent or company.

Nevertheless, should the homebuyers decide to use the real-estate company's in-house lender, the homebuyers need to be made aware of the fact that the in-house lender will usually be working on a smaller commission basis until their loan closures reach a bonus-point structure, that is established by their company based on the company's monthly loan funding. When their bonus-point structure is reached, the in-house lender will be making the same amount of commissions as the other lenders that are not associated or affiliated with a real-estate company.

So what does all of this mean to homebuyers? Homebuyers will usually end up paying more for their home loan with an in-house lender then they would normally pay with another lender that is not associated with or affiliated with a real-estate company. The reason for this is that the other lenders do not have to worry about making a quota in order to make their commissions, whereas an in-house lender will charge the homebuyers more in points for their loan to compensate them for their smaller commissions, or they will offer the homebuyers a higher interest rate with no points up front, knowing that they will be compensated handsomely by the lenders in the form of rebate points. Furthermore, seldom if ever will in-house lenders achieve monthly loan funding in the amounts established by their companies in order to be compensated in the form of bonus points. Therefore, someone is going to pay, and unfortunately you, the homebuyers, are the considerable amount of money who will pay if buyers are not aware of this information.

Another organization that is notorious for directing homebuyers to their lenders is New Home Developments. This is basically because of the same reasons stated earlier. In this situation, if the homebuyers believe that they can get better financing than what the New Home Development on-site real-estate agents are offering, they should seek out those lenders. Caution! It is not uncommon for a Home Development or their on-site real-estate agents to attempt to coerce potential homebuyers into using their financing by informing the homebuyers that they *must* provide financial approval from another lender in a very short period of time or they will lose their home. They may even deny the homebuyers the credit incentives if they use another lender, or they may charge the homebuyers a per diem fee for each day the homebuyers are late in closing, which is not done to the homebuyers if the homebuyers use their on-site lender. These tactics used by New Home Developers and their on-site real-estate agents is technically not against the law that I know of, but it usually causes the homebuyers to submit to using the New Home Developers on-site real-estate agents' financing. Should this happen to any potential homebuyers, feel free to call the Office of Thrift Supervision (OTS), or the Office of the Comptrollers of the Currency (OCC), or the Department of Real Estate in your state, and inform them as to the demands that are being made on you by New Home Developers or their on-site real-estate agents concerning the purchase of one of the Developers homes. Once reported, an investigation will follow by the appropriate agencies immediately, and I can assure the homebuyers that the situation will be resolved to the homebuyers' benefit in a very short period of time. However, allow me to clarify some terminology. The words *directing* or *suggesting* would probably be more appropriate here, as *steering* is against the law.

How do homebuyers get around this situation? Simple; first of all, ask the real-estate agent who recommends their in-house lender to also recommend at least two more lenders that you can make comparisons with, or tell your real-estate agent that you intend to check with other lenders before making a decision. At this point, homebuyers will want to be careful, because most real-estate agents will attempt to inform you that you only have seven days in order to apply for a home loan, which is indicated in the purchase contract unless the sellers agree to ten days or X number of days, that will be written into the contract or agreement if that is the case. This is basically the same tactics New Home Development Companies and their on-site real-estate agent's use. *Don't*—I repeat—*don't* fall into this trap. Simply inform the real-estate agent that you believe, according to the Department of Real Estate, that as a homebuyer you have the right to seek your own home financing, and then ask the real-estate agent if this is true. If you get a positive answer, fine. However, if he or she says "What if. . .," "What happens when. . .," "But we can. . .," etc., ask the real-estate agent to explain to you what *steering means*, or ask him/her if you can discuss this with the office manager or the office broker. It is guaranteed that you will get a positive response at this point in time.

Even though I mentioned this previously, log this into your memory banks: Real-estate mortgage loan consultants, loan officers, and lenders in the state of California and most other states must be licensed in order to conduct real-estate business, and the only exception to this licensing requirement applies only to loan officers who work for or are under the direction of a federal savings-and-loan institution or bank, which incidentally, are now also requiring some of their loan officers to be real estate licensed. Furthermore, because loan officers and most lenders are licensed in real estate, they have the same knowledge that the real-estate agents have, and they are extremely familiar with the rules and regulations of the Department of Real Estate. Therefore, it is my professional recommendation that homebuyers talk to lenders other than the one to whom the real-estate agent referred you. Regardless of which lender you decide to do business with, be sure they have the homebuyer's best interest at hand, and not their hands in the homebuyer's pocketbook!

Yes, it will cost the homebuyers money to get a home loan, and yes, most lenders do work on a straight commission basis, and yes, they deserve to be paid just like you or anyone else. The only question is, how much? As you have already read, not nearly as much as a real-estate agent will make on any one particular transaction, but by the same token, homebuyers should expect a fair deal from their mortgage loan consultant, loan officer, or lender, depending upon the homebuyer's particular circumstances. Remember, everything is negotiable in real-estate transactions!

Do You Recommend Contacting a Lender First to Pre-qualify?

Yes, most definitely, and here is why. In today's marketplace, homebuyers who have advance knowledge and notification of their purchasing and/or financial abilities will definitely place themselves above those homebuyers who do not know what they can qualify for in the way of a home purchase because they will not know or have the proper knowledge of their purchasing and/or financing capabilities. On the other hand, having this knowledge will help the real-estate agents and allow the homebuyers to view properties in the price range that they are qualified to purchase. Homebuyers may also want to inform the real-estate agents that they have been pre-qualified by their lender, and they may want to indicate to them what their down payment may be, depending on the price of the home they decide to purchase. Homebuyers may also want to inform the real-estate agents that they intend to purchase a property within X number of days or weeks, depending upon whether or not their real-estate agent has properties available in their price range.

Nonetheless, the homebuyers will want to show the real-estate agents some sort of financial documentation from their lender that will verify their financial abilities, as well as to demonstrate their knowledge and sincerity that they are, in fact, able and willing to make a purchase. Likewise, the financial documentation needs to be signed by the bank's loan division officer or by someone in the bank's loan division to add to their creditability. Finally, should the homebuyers be satisfied that their real-estate agent will assist and work for them they should give the real-estate agent their word that they will not shop with other real-estate agents. The reason for stating this to the real-estate agent is to give the homebuyers the advantage of having an exclusive real-estate agent that will trust them, and will work even harder to satisfy their wants and needs. And finally, when homebuyers are able to present prequalification financial documentation from a bank or lender to the real-estate agent, this will usually put a stop to being directed or suggested to use another lender by the agent, which can eliminate a lot of potential problems.

Is There Any Such Thing as a Loan Approval or Loan Pre-approval?

Yes and No. Let's start with the yes. The homebuyers who have their financial documentation viewed and signed by an officer of the loan division of a direct lender or bank are classified as having a loan pre-approval that is technically a guarantee of the homebuyer's financial ability to purchase a home. At the same time, it still does not guarantee that the homebuyer has met all the criteria required in order to be granted a home loan by a bank or any other direct lender.

Let's look at the "no" aspect of a loan pre-approval. The idea of a loan approval, whether verbal or written, is a major misconception that has and will probably continue to plague the real-estate industry because of a lack of knowledge on the part of the real-estate agents that has been caused by the lending industry. There is no such thing as a verbal or a written loan pre-approval that has any validity whatsoever should it be issued by a mortgage loan consultant, loan officer, or any other lender. The only exception is a signed loan pre-approval from a bank or another direct lender, which will only indicate the homebuyer's financial ability to purchase a home of a particular value. The final decision will not be made until all of the lender's loan approval criteria have been met by the homebuyer.

As a multi-million-dollar loan officer, I have given both verbal and written loan pre-approvals to real-estate agents only to satisfy their requests that they wrote in their real-estate purchase contracts and receipts for deposit. However, it should be noted, that what real-estate agents write in the Purchase Contract and Receipt for Deposit means absolutely nothing to lenders. A loan pre-approval is nothing more than a fallacy that has been created by the lending institutions. However, there is a valid reason for the lending institutions to have created this fallacy, which was designed not only to create a favorable impression on the real-estate agents, but also to satisfy a real-estate agent's seller's psychological insecurities.

The primary reason that the lenders started to use the terms *loan approval* or *loan pre-approval* was to gain the business of the real-estate agents. Lenders assumed that if they were to offer or issue real-estate agents a loan approval or loan pre-approval, whether verbal or written, the real-estate agents, as well as the homebuyers, would stop shopping around for another lender. Likewise, if the lender could convince the real-estate agents that they should request a loan approval or loan pre-approval from their homebuyers, the real-estate agents' sales transactions would increase and be secured. Unfortunately, this is not true, and unfortunately, the lenders were right, in that the real-estate agents bought it hook, line, and sinker!

Whether you are a home seller or a homebuyer, this is very important to remember: a lender is under no obligation whatsoever when issuing a verbal or written loan approval or loan pre-approval. The lenders cannot be held liable, nor is there any recourse against lenders who have issued a loan approval or loan pre-approval whether verbal, written, or otherwise! Why? Because lenders are under no obligation to grant homebuyers a home loan or grant homebuyers a commitment to make a home loan until the homebuyers meet all of the lender's requirements regarding credit, appraisal, documentation verification, confirmation of terms, continued program availability, and any other terms or conditions that a lender may require from the homebuyers. In other words, yes, there is such a thing as a loan approval or loan pre-approval that can be issued by a bank or another direct lender, but this can only be done concerning the financial credibility and purchasing ability of potential homebuyers. Other than that, there is no such thing as a loan approval or loan pre-approval.

As a homebuyer, or for that matter a real-estate agent, ask yourself this question: If a bank or any other direct or non-direct lender was to issue a verbal or written loan approval or loan pre-approval concerning any homebuyer's financial credibility and purchasing ability without requiring any additional information or criteria, what do you think would happen to these lenders? Would they be put out of business? Would the OTS shut them down? Would they go to jail? A combination of all of the above would probably take place. So now homebuyers know the truth about loan approvals and loan pre-approvals.

Are There Hidden Costs in Getting a Home Loan?

As a rule, reputable lenders will not have hidden costs, or "garbage fees," as they are known in the lending industry. However, there are additional fees that will be required in order to secure a home loan. As was previously mentioned, homebuyers will have nonrecurring closing costs, which include the lender and broker fees indicated in a good faith estimate or California's mortgage loan disclosure statement (MLDS). Likewise, there will be third-party fees, which will include, but not be limited to: private mortgage insurance fees, (if the homebuyer's down payment is less than 20%), escrow fees, processing fees, underwriting fees, recording fees, notary fees, title insurance fees, documentary transfer tax fees (purchases only), tax service fees (only on a refinanced loan that has new monies involved), document fees, messenger fees, discount point fees, review appraisal fees, and or other fees depending on the fees charged by the homebuyer's particular lender and the state the homebuyer is located in. All of these fees will be indicated in California's MLDS or a good faith estimate, one of which all homebuyers will receive. Furthermore, because all of these fees are tax deductible in the year that they are paid (on home purchases only), be sure to keep a copy of the good faith statement and the closing statement/HUD1 for your records.

In addition, as I mentioned earlier, lenders will require up-front credit and appraisal fees. Normally, the only fees that homebuyers are required to pay up front are for their credit and appraisal reports. However, caution is in order here, as some lenders may require $1,000 or more in up front fees. The reason some lenders and brokers attempt to request large up-front fees is in anticipation of stopping the prospective homebuyers from shopping for a better loan from other mortgage lenders. Likewise, these are usually the lenders and brokers who have poor loan closing ratios. Furthermore, lenders and brokers who want to charge up-front fees must now be approved by the Department of Real Estate in the state of California before they can charge these fees. Nonetheless, should this happen in any particular home-buying situation, it is my suggestion that the homebuyers may want to locate another lender in their marketplace, as all homebuyers have a right to shop for the best mortgage-interest-rate home loan. Furthermore, and as a rule, credit reports in California are currently $15.00 for a single person and $32.00 to $45.00 per couple. Appraisal fees will range between $450 and up depending on the size and value of the home the homebuyers are attempting to purchase as of the year 2015.

Nevertheless, unless the homebuyers have some serious personal circumstances, e.g., bankruptcy, a history of collections, judgments, notices of default (NOD), non-verifiable income, or high debit ratios, their total nonrecurring closing cost and third-party fees should not exceed 4 % (+ or -) of the total loan amount that the homebuyers are financing, assuming that their mortgage loan consultant or loan officer is quoting the homebuyers an interest-rate loan that is on par. In other words, there is no cost to the lender to buy the homebuyers' interest rate from a wholesale lender that would consider financing their home mortgage loan. Moreover, should the homebuyers like to receive a lower interest rate than they were quoted, the homebuyers must realize that the lender is going to have to charge more points, simply because it will cost the lender more money to buy the lower interest rate from the wholesale lender. This is known as a *"Rate Fee Buy-Down."* Finally, I would also like to point out to the homebuyers that they have the right to question any and all fees that they may be subject to paying, and they also have the ability to negotiate each and every fee being quoted. Likewise, and even though I have stated this before, homebuyers need to remember, everything is negotiable in real estate transactions!

What Are Garbage Fees? And Do They Still Exist?

Garbage fees can be classified as being borderline legal or illegal gray-area fees that are charged to the unsuspecting homebuyers by escrow and title companies as well as the lenders, and yes, they still exist. It is also interesting to note that the lenders who have qualified and have been approved and authorized by the government to grant FHA and VA loans cannot charge homebuyers garbage fees, and yet the banks and other lenders in the conventional loan marketplace can still get away with charging these fees. Garbage fees can come under all sorts of different classifications, and they can cost the unsuspecting homebuyer hundreds, if not thousands of dollars more, as long as the terminology being expounded by these nettlesome varlets sounds official.

Let's look at some typical garbage fee classifications, and keep in mind that all or any of these fees can be negotiated down or even eliminated, providing the homebuyers know what to look for and have the ability to question the escrow and title companies and the lenders about these garbage fees before signing any loan documentation. All of the following are garbage fee classifications: underwriter review fee (conventional), subsidy fee, lender's inspection fee, assignment fee, loan fee paid to broker/creditor, warehouse fee, advance commitment fee, document redraw fee (charged if borrowers make a change, but not charged if the error is made by the bank), trustee fee, legal review fee, survey fee, bank funding fee, lender's approval fee, loan tie-in fee, and sub-escrow fees. Furthermore, there are also semi-garbage fees, that are legitimate fees in which the charges can be quite excessive, and they are as follows: wire transfer fees, recording fees, and messenger fees. Now, even though these are legitimate fees, wire transfer fees can be as high as $200 for a $15 to $25 cost. I have seen recording fees as high as $175 for a $9 cost (one page of 8½ × 11 sheet of paper) plus $3 in direct cost for each additional page being recorded, or a total cost of $54 for recording a sixteen-page deed of trust. I have seen messenger fees as high as $150 for supposedly taking a deed of trust to the county recorder's office for recording, and I have seen the same charge being applied without even having or using a messenger.

Remember, homebuyers must be able to stand their ground and listen to the BS (Blue Sky) explanations they will receive from whomever they are questioning about these fees. Moreover, homebuyers should not be afraid to or even hesitate to disagree with the lender's explanations to the point, that the lender will reluctantly reduce the garbage fees or eliminate them altogether should the lender believe or think that the homebuyers may back out of the loan. Likewise, these garbage fee classifications will not be limited as long as there are people in the lending industry who are capable of conjuring up any additional terminology that sounds official in order to extract or extort additional monies from the unsuspecting homebuyers as long as there is money to be made by the companies involved in any given mortgage loan transaction.

Allow me to give you an example of an escrow closing I attended years ago. I was assisting a young lady who was buying a new home with her mortgage loan when I received a call from her asking me if I would meet with her for the escrow closing, where she would be signing the final loan documentation, and I agreed. Upon arriving at the escrow office, I informed my client not to indicate who I was to the escrow officer so as not to put this person in an uncomfortable position. My client agreed, and we went into the escrow company. After we were seated, the escrow officer began explaining the various forms to my client, who continued to sign them until we came to the closing statement and the good faith statement. As I started to go over the various charges with the client, I noticed several garbage fee classifications, whereupon I immediately started questioning the escrow officer as to the validity of the charges. After listening to the escrow officer's explanation, I informed her that we disagreed with the charges and therefore would not sign the documentation to finalize the home transaction. The escrow officer excused herself, and when she returned, she brought the owner with her, who also attempted to persuade my client into signing. Again we refused, and finally the charges were eliminated.

One of the charges I questioned the escrow company about was the loan tie-in fee. I asked the escrow officer to explain how the company had managed to tie in a loan fee. Naturally, there was no such thing, and hence no loan tie-in fee. Next, we questioned the sub-escrow fee, only to find out that this fee was being charged by the title company. Therefore, we called the title company and asked them if their office had a basement where they conducted a "sub-escrow." Naturally, there was no basement, and hence no "sub-escrow." As I continued to question the various garbage fees, the escrow officer started to become more and more evasive, even to the point where she indicated that several of the garbage fees were being charged by the lender. When I heard this statement I asked the escrow officer to place a call to the lender so that I could verify this information. The escrow officer stated that calling the lender was not her responsibility, at which point I informed her that I was the mortgage loan consultant on this transaction and further informed her that if she did not place a call to the lender, my client would be happy to call the State of California Commissioner's Office and report their noncompliance.

Now, to make a long story short and to the point, the lender had not charged the garbage fees the escrow officer claimed they had, and when all the documentation was signed and finalized, my client received a check for $1,800.00 after the close of escrow. Not bad for spending a couple of hours disputing and disagreeing with garbage fees. Nevertheless, should the homebuyers not understand or suspect that there are garbage fees being charged in their home transaction, they should feel free to question the charges until those charges are eliminated or reduced to a reasonable level. Incidentally, the lady in this story became my wife a few years later.

What Are Credit Scores? And Can They Affect Mortgage Rates?

In today's world, credit scores are used by just about everyone who would like to know how creditworthy a person is according to a scoring model. A credit score, also known as a FICO score, has been designed—in theory anyway—to attempt to grade or score a person based on their ability to borrow money and repay it in a timely manner. The models used to assist in making this determination were based on the compilation of information that had been accumulated from millions of credit reports in order to narrow down the information into the most important categories that would most likely assist in determining a person's ability to borrow monies and repay their obligations. Once this information was narrowed down, a statistical mathematical model was designed to correlate all of this information and compose a scoring model that works on a scale that runs from 300 to 850 based on the analysis of this information and is supposed to determine the risk of extending credit to potential borrowers.

The most used statistical mathematical model in use today is from the Fair Isaac Corporation, which is traded on the NYSC under the symbol FIC. The company was founded in 1956 by engineer Bill Fair and mathematician Earl Isaac, and as ironic as it may be, the credit scoring model they developed was designed to attempt to quantify the likelihood that a prospective borrower would fail to repay a loan or other credit obligation satisfactorily over a specific given period of time. The reason that this is peculiar is that one would think the scoring model would be more likely to determine the likelihood that a prospective borrower would have the ability to repay a loan or other credit obligation as opposed to failing to repay. Nevertheless, this is the most widely used scoring model currently being used by lenders, banks, credit card companies, insurance companies, and any company doing business with the general public in which credit may be offered to customers.

Let's now look at what makes up the credit score or FICO score, and keep in mind that the scores and their variables were designed to determine the risk of default based on the statistical mathematical model. Moreover, because the exact formula for calculating the credit score or FICO score is a closely guarded secret, Fair Isaac has disclosed the following components, along with the approximate weighted contribution of each:

35% of the scoring is based on the punctuality of payments made in the past; this is also known as a person's payment history. Remember, it is better to make payments early than late for scoring purposes, and if necessary, make a lesser payment if one has to instead of the full payment, as the payment counts when recorded even though it is not the correct amount.

30% is based on current balances of revolving debt, such as credit cards, and it is calculated on a ratio of total available revolving credit limits vs. the current balance. In the mortgage industry, homebuyers and homeowners who intend to refinance will want to be sure to stay under 75% of their maximum allowable credit limit, as anything over this percentage will cause lenders to look twice at your credit. Also, being just $1 over the 100% limit can cause a drop of 100 points in a person's credit score or FICO score. If possible, keep the revolving credit expenditures in the 50% to 65% range, but definitely keep them under 75% if looking for a mortgage loan and that means *all* revolving credit.

15% is based on the total length of time a person has had credit, and it is referred to as credit history. The longer a person maintains his or her credit, the better it is as viewed from the standpoint of the prospective lender or extender of credit. Therefore, if a person has an old credit card, and even if they don't use it anymore, it is better to keep the card as opposed to canceling it, as this is used as part of the statistical mathematical model to determine a person's overall credit history. For example, let's say a person started his/her credit history with a credit card when in his/her late teens or early twenties, and twenty years later he/she still has that same credit card. This person would be viewed as being a better credit risk than, let's say, a millionaire who has paid cash for everything they ever wanted over the same period of time, and then suddenly decided to purchase something on credit. The millionaire would be considered a high-risk person because they never established a credit history that would satisfy a lender or extender of credit. So, keeping an open line of credit is far better than having no credit history at all.

10% of the credit score is based on the types of credit extended to a person in the past as well as recently, such as revolving credit cards, installment payments, car loans, mortgages, open and closed accounts, etc. It is also important to realize that accounts charging no interest or finance charges should the item be paid for in a set period of time will have no effect on a person's credit score if the item is paid off. However, should a person not elect to pay off such an account and allow the interest to be applied and amortized over a given period of time, then the offering and the item would be considered an installment payment and would become part of the scoring process.

Last but not least, 10% of the scoring is based on recent credit extended—the amount of credit issued or received as well as the number of inquiries that were made concerning a person's credit assessment. This score will be based on everything I just explained as well as the inquiries made by companies to determine a person's creditworthiness. As a rule, any inquiries that are made concerning a person's credit will not have much of an impact on their credit scoring providing the inquiries do not exceed ten or more per year, and not all ten in one month. In my professional opinion, the number of inquiries made concerning any given person should not have any effect whatsoever on a person's credit score, as the majority of credit inquiries are made without the consent or knowledge of the person who maintains the credit. Furthermore, I consider the inquiry aspect used in the statistical mathematical model to be flawed and out of place concerning the credit scoring of any given person, especially without their verbal or written consent and acknowledgement. As long as a person does not have an open account and has not requested credit be pulled, the person has a right to place a complaint, as that company is in violation of the Privacy Act Law and the company can be fined.

This category could be a book all by itself, but because I have more important information to relate to the readers, I will only take a little more time in showing homebuyers the credit scores they will need in order to qualify for a home loan. Should the reader desire to learn or know more about credit and the credit scoring process, there is a myriad of sources of information to be accessed on the World Wide Web, so feel free to browse the web.

In the mortgage lending industry, credit reports are referred to as paper, and there are paper classifications known as A and A-, B, C, D, and E-paper, which determine the creditworthiness of the homebuyers and also determine the type of mortgage loan they would be able to qualify for when applying for a home loan. Over the years the paper classifications have changed, and they are no longer referred to as A and A-, B, C, D, and E-paper, but rather A-paper and sub-prime paper that also no longer exist in today's mortgage market. Currently, there is no longer any real subprime or "A" paper loans available as they are all rolled into one loan product. However, there are portfolio products out there that are close to sub-prime, but not with the same guidelines that used to be used that caused the financial debacle, and is pretty much referred to as manual underwritten loans. There is also an automated underwriting system (AUS) that 99.9 percent of files are run through today, and there are no stated income document loans available that we know of in the current market place. However, there are alternative income documentation loans starting to show up, but they are requiring 24 month bank statements. Furthermore, the present mortgage lender market is primarily FHA, VA, and Conventional FNMA/FHLMC, and USDA lenders. Likewise, the FHA and VA minimum FICO is around 580, but the majority of lenders require a FICO score between 600 or 620, and the conventional standard minimum FICO score is around 620; although a few lenders will consider going lower, but they are far and few between in the lending market place.

Now, homebuyers that currently have a sub-prime mortgage-interest-rate loans need to pay special attention to what I am going to relate, as it could be the difference of keeping or losing a home in two or three years. As I indicated earlier, these sub-prime loans were designed to assist homebuyers with bad credit to give them an opportunity to purchase, and get into a home with the understanding that they will clear up their bad credit, and be able to qualify for an a better mortgage-interest-rate loan before the sub-prime loan converts, or makes the adjustment from a fixed-interest-rate loan to an adjustable-interest-rate loan. However, should the homebuyers not take the time to clear up their bad credit in the allotted time period then I suggest that the homebuyers sell their home. Moreover, should the homebuyers decide not to sell their home, they will need to prepare themselves for foreclosure proceedings—unless, of course, they get an inheritance or win the lotto. As I stated earlier, these are very dangerous mortgage loans, and if allowed to convert, the homebuyers will be faced with major monthly mortgage payment increases with ridiculous, ludicrous margins and lifetime caps, and it will then be just a matter of time before they lose their homes. Therefore, and even though it may be difficult, take the 2-3 years to clear up your credit and get yourself a better mortgage-interest-rate loan.

There are several different ways to clear up a person's credit in order to improve his or her overall credit/FICO scores. Homebuyers can repair their own credit if they have the time and patience, as this process can take anywhere from six months to a year or longer in order to clear up their credit. Furthermore, everyone is entitled to one free credit report from each of the credit reporting agencies each and every year, as long as it has been a full twelve months since receiving the last free credit report, but homebuyers should understand that these credit reports may not include their Credit/FICO scores. Therefore, if you are one of those persons who would like to take the time to clear up your own credit, then be sure to ask if the free credit report includes the credit/FICO score. If it does, great; and if it doesn't, then you will have to seek out another source to get your credit report that has the credit/FICO scores, otherwise you will be getting mostly useless information.

The next approach for clearing up credit is to seek out a Credit Counseling Organization that is offering their services free of charge. These organizations may also take a while to clear up the homebuyer's credit, but the time may be well worth the wait. Another approach for the homebuyers would be to contact and use a credit repair company, as these organizations specialize in the area of credit repair. However, be sure to get as many references as possible from the companies you may consider doing business with, as the field of credit repair is replete with fly-by-niters and the results are not guaranteed, so you could end up not having your credit repaired and eventually lose a considerable amount of money at the same time. Nevertheless, in my professional opinion, using credit repair companies having personnel with legal or paralegal backgrounds would be a safer approach for the homebuyers. Likewise, another approach would be to use an attorney or an attorney service specializing in credit clearing. These organizations will normally charge for their services, but like everything else, these fees can be negotiated.

Another approach that I have used over the years, that is basically an insider's secret, and little known to the general public, is to use a loan company's processor or an independent processing company's processor, especially if the processor was the one who put the home loan package together for the homebuyers. Why? Simple; they already know everything there is to know about the homebuyers. That information is tucked away in some loan box that is stuck in some closet somewhere for the next four years, which incidentally, is the same period of time required for the Statue of Fraud to expire in a mortgage transaction.

Now, if the homebuyers do not remember who the processor was, they can simply call the mortgage loan consultant, loan officer or lender and ask that person for the name, and if they want to know why you want to know the processor's name, simply tell them that you want to thank this person for assisting you with your home loan. Once you have the processor's name, give them a call and thank them for assisting with your home loan, and then ask them if they would consider assisting you with clearing up your credit, stating that you will gladly pay them for their services. Over the years of being in the loan business, I have used this approach several times with excellent results, as most processors are happy to be able to assist with credit clearing, and being able to make some extra money at the same time.

SECTION 2: COST AND RATES

What Are Rates, and How Are They Determined?

Rates are nothing more than interest rates that are quoted to the homebuyers by the mortgage loan consultant or loan officer. Because this process is extremely complex, I will attempt to give the homebuyers a general overview of how the system works concerning the establishment of interest rates. The Federal Reserve Board of the United States is the direct culprit when it comes to establishing and determining what our nation's interest rates will be on any given day, 365 days a year. The Fed decides if the banking lending rates should be increased or decreased based on the current state of the country's economy. This means that the interest rates being quoted by the Fed are the interest rates that the banks have to pay in order to be able to borrow money from the Federal Reserve. Once the Fed interest rate figure is announced, the banks borrow money as they deem necessary, and in turn, the banks lend these monies out to the general public in the form of loans.

Next the banks use their own formulas to establish the interest rates that the general public would be required to pay in the event that they would like to borrow money, which naturally is going to be considerably more interest than what the banks are paying to borrow the same money from the Fed.

Because the economy is constantly changing, this is the reason that the interest-rate market is constantly changing, thereby keeping the economy in balance with the rest of the world. In addition, the investors who purchase mortgage loans in the secondary mortgage market will affect interest rates. These investors will quote the direct lenders the net yield that they will require in order to purchase a mortgage loan in the secondary market, and if the direct lenders cannot sell their mortgage loans because the yield is too low, the direct lenders will be forced to continue servicing the loans, which means sending out mortgage statements and collecting the payments until such a time that the quoted yield comes down to or moves up to the point that the direct lenders are able to sell their mortgage loans. On the other hand, lenders will increase their home loan interest rates in order to increase the loan's yield to the point at which they will be able to sell their mortgage loans in the secondary mortgage market. Furthermore, if a direct lender intends to service the homebuyer's mortgage for a while before selling the loan in the secondary market, the lender will usually add anywhere from .250 to .375 of a percent to service the loan, thereby increasing the net yield on the homebuyer's mortgage until such a time the direct lender decides to sell the loan in the secondary mortgage market.

Are There Home Loan Indicators Concerning Interest Rates?

Yes and no, my personal recommendation is to buy the *Wall Street Journal,* as it will indicate what the Federal National Mortgage Association, AKA Fannie Mae (FNMA) and the Federal Home Loan Mortgage Corporation, AKA Freddie Mac (FHLMC) will do to the interest rates each and every day. Note: FNMA and FHLMC are no longer affiliated with the United States government and are in fact the largest private mortgage loan buyers in the secondary mortgage market. However, unless the homebuyers are major real-estate investors (investing large sums of money monthly), the majority of homebuyers will want to consider viewing the bond market or calling their local bank or mortgage loan broker's office or view the Internet for the current home loan interest rates being offered and quoted in their given areas of the country. Note: Caution is in order here, because the homebuyers may or may not receive the proper information from the person that they will be talking to, and they may or may not be getting the current up-to-date information concerning interest rates they view over the Internet. Regardless of whether or not the homebuyers are viewing the Internet or speaking to a mortgage loan consultant or loan officer, they should remember that they will only be getting basic information concerning what interest rates may or may not be doing at any given point in time.

Allow me to point out the facts of life concerning mortgage loan consultants and loan officers: The longevity of a new mortgage loan officer is approximately ninety days in the mortgage loan business. Why? Because the lending institutions advertise that anyone can make a minimum of $5,000 or more per month every month within a period of three months or so in the mortgage loan business. Unfortunately, this is not only a pure fantasy, but also pure (and I am going to be polite here) Blue Sky known as BS in my vernacular. I have pointed this out in my real-estate sales manual, which I wrote for the real-estate industry in California, in the section entitled "Lenders," under the caption, "Time in the Business."

Time in the mortgage loan business may not seem like much or mean very much to the prospective homebuyers, but the very outcome of their transactions may well depend on the amount of experience that a homebuyer's mortgage loan officer has in the mortgage loan business. Now, don't take this the wrong way or misunderstand, as a new mortgage loan officer may in fact be a very capable person and one who may be able to assist the homebuyers with their home loan transactions, providing that the new mortgage loan officer has sufficient backing from their in-house personnel.

Nonetheless, because the turnover rate of a new mortgage loan officer is approximately 90% in ninety days or so, homebuyers may want to consider a seasoned pro known as a loan consultant who has survived for at least one year in the mortgage loan business. Three years is better, five years is great, and ten plus years is fantastic, for these mortgage loan consultants must be doing something right, i.e., closing homebuyers loans! On the other hand, should the homebuyers encounter a new mortgage loan officer who is willing to give the homebuyers the name and direct phone line of their mortgage loan manager, then the homebuyers should feel comfortable in knowing that additional loan assistance is available from the head honcho of the mortgage loan division. Nevertheless, homebuyers should not hesitate to ask their mortgage loan consultant or loan officer how long they have been in the loan business. Remember, experience is gained from knowledge, and knowledge is gained from trial and error and time! All anyone has to do is look at their own office and note the successful people. What do they all have in common? Knowledge with Time in the business!

This information is very important to understand, so pay attention. There are a myriad of different mortgage loans available in the home loan marketplace, which will be discussed further on. However, other than the standard, simplistic rip-off fixed-rate loans that are available, all of the other loans available in the mortgage-loan market need to be understood and explained in their entirety so that there will be no misunderstandings as to the inner workings of these mortgage loans. To explain this information another way, if the homebuyers mortgage loan consultant or loan officer recommends any loan to the homebuyers other than a standard fixed-rate loan, they had better have the knowledge and expertise to be able to explain these mortgage loan programs in their entirety to their clients. Likewise, the homebuyers must have a complete understanding of the inner working aspects of these loans so that they will not become subjected to filing for bankruptcy three to five years down the road.

Furthermore, because these mortgage loans are extremely complicated and complex in their functions, homebuyers who do not fully understand these loans will find themselves in serious trouble as their loan progresses in time. Even though these other mortgage loans are far superior to the standard fixed-rate loans, they need to be understood by the homebuyers, and if it takes a couple of weeks or more to understand the inner workings of these loans, then so be it, and in the event that the homebuyers don't understand the inner workings of a loan, the homebuyers should not sign the loan documentation. Likewise, the mortgage loan consultant or loan officer who recommends one of these mortgage loans to the homebuyers had better have the knowledge, experience, and expertise to be able to explain the inner workings of these loans in their entirety. So, as you can now see, it can take years for a mortgage loan consultant or loan officer to be able to understand the inner workings of just two or three of these complex loans, let alone the multitude of the mortgage loans that are available in the mortgage loan marketplace.

As a multi-million-dollar loan consultant, I constantly checked approximately thirty-two to thirty-five different financial indicators and observed worldly events on a daily basis in order to advise my home-buying clients as to the best mortgage loans and interest rates currently available, in addition to advising the homebuyers as to what the interest rates might do within a few days or weeks depending on what these indicators were indicating. However, and as a rule, if there is not a major move in interest rates, homebuyers do not need to be too concerned. Be sure to note that in the event of a major interest-rate move, the local television news network will definitely let the homebuyers know, so watch the news.

Likewise, it also took me several years as a mortgage loan consultant to learn and understand some of these additional mortgage loan programs that are available in the marketplace. In fact, it took me twelve years just to understand the inner workings of one of the most complicated, complex, and most feared loan programs available in the mortgage market, which turned out to be the best mortgage loan available anywhere in the entire United States. And yet, the lending institutions are issuing this mortgage loan to approximately 80 to 90 percent of all homebuyers in the state of California, as well as other states without having the slightest idea of what the inner workings of this loan are and how this loan works, let alone being able to explain this loan to the homebuyers. This mortgage loan happened to be the best mortgage loan on the market, and it is known as the negative, or option, loan. We will be covering, dissecting, and unraveling the complexity of this loan in extensive detail in order to show these 80 to 90 percent homebuyers in California and in the other states how to turn the tables on the lending institutions and how to use this loan to manipulate the banks and drive them crazy! Current update: The Negative Adjustable or Option loan is no longer available in the mortgage loan marketplace at this time because this loan was the major cause of the financial crisis that the United States went through in this country along other greedy countries causing a massive financial disruption. However, in time, it is possible for the negative adjustable to return to the mortgage loan marketplace, and especially, when the home buying public starts learning and understanding the advantages only this loan can offer any homebuyers. Nevertheless, it will up the homebuyers to keep requesting and demanding that the lenders bring back the negative adjustable loan.

Does the Stock Market Affect Interest Rates?

No. The activity of the stock market only has an indirect effect on interest rates. As indicated earlier, there are approximately thirty-two to thirty-five different financial indicators that can indirectly affect what may or may not happen to the interest-rate market. However, none of these financial indicators will give homebuyers a direct indication as to how interest rates will perform from day to day, and unless the homebuyers are in the mortgage loan business, these indicators and their information would be of little use and value. Nonetheless, as a real-estate lender, I used to watch the bond market, and based on the activity of the bond market and its yield, I could tell homebuyers what interest rates would be doing from day to day with extreme accuracy.

Now that I have given you one of my trade secrets, allow me to give you the basic theory of economics, which states the following: In the event there is concern of future inflation, interest rates will go up. , there are some additional indicators that will have an effect on interest rates here in the United States; these factors have to do with world events. However, unless homebuyers know how to read these events and indicators, they should not be too concerned with what interest rates may or may not be doing, as I am sure homebuyers have a lot more important things to be concerned about in their daily activities.

Furthermore, until homebuyers are ready to make a home purchase or refinance their homes, being concerned about what interest may or may not be doing may only cause homebuyers unnecessary stress. Therefore, when homebuyers are ready to purchase or refinance a home, their best source of financial information concerning current interest rates will be the daily newspaper, the *Wall Street Journal,* or the Internet, as well as a good qualified seasoned mortgage loan consultant.

Would It Be Better to Wait for Rates to Go Down before We Buy a Home?

This depends on whether homebuyers are buying a home or a mortgage loan. My recommendation is that prospective homebuyers should buy a home when they can afford it and not wait for the rates to go down. If the homebuyers wait for rates to go down, the question becomes, how low do the rates have to go before they feel confident to buy? On the other hand, if rates are high, it usually is an indicator that there is fear of future inflation. However, by waiting to see what rates may or may not do, prospective homebuyers may be putting themselves in an inflationary cycle. A good point to remember is that a good mortgage loan consultant or loan officer will have access to several loan programs which can be customized to meet the prospective homebuyer's needs. So, if homebuyers can afford to buy, they should buy, otherwise the home they want, desire, and deserve may not be available if the homebuyers decide to wait and see what interest rates will do.

However, there is also a reverse thought to take into consideration, which is, in the event that the home market should reach a point of saturation or a level of unjustified appreciation, which would cause the average homebuyers the inability to purchase a home, then I would suggest to the prospective homebuyers to wait, as a major setback or home market decline may very well be on the near horizon. The last time this event took place in the state of California was back in 1982, when the home market declined a little over 50 percent, at which time prospective homebuyers could buy million-dollar homes for half price or less. Moreover, as of this writing, we are currently in a direct parallel in 2008 with what was occurring in 1980 and 1981 in the California real-estate market just before the home market declined. Likewise, I do not expect to see any major turn-a-round in the housing market until 2020 or later as the US economy doesn't have or maintain any sufficient economical forward movements or developments at this time that could catapult the US into a new and vibrant recovery.

Interest rates are moving up, and housing appreciation has been unjustified, and way out of line according to the standard appreciation tables here in California, where property usually doubles in value every eight years, or at twelve and a half percent annually. Oil has gone haywire, the energy crisis has never been completely resolved in California, and it has been over twenty-four years since the last major home market decline. Furthermore, the housing market is at the 18.5-trillion-dollar mark, or the equivalent to that of the stock market in the year 2000 just before it crashed, and the housing market alone has generated over 6.5 trillion dollars within the last two years. In this particular situation here in California, if homebuyers were to ask me what they should do concerning the purchasing of a home or refinancing, I would advise them to wait for another year before purchasing a home, and I would advise the homebuyers who are thinking about refinancing to refinance now while interest rates are still relatively low as they currently are in 2015. Likewise, the oil prices are rapidly declining in 2015 that are also causing gas prices to plummet, and may even get down to $1.50 or less per gallon, and as to how long the public will be able to enjoy these gas prices is anyone's guess.

Even though this situation occurs infrequently, it still occurs, and prospective homebuyers need to make themselves aware of what is going on in the housing market. The wrong move at the wrong time in the real estate home market can have devastating consequences for homebuyers for years to come, and unless homebuyers are capable of weathering the fallout in the housing market, they will be forced into bankruptcy. The recovery period from the housing decline in 1982 took eight years, and the next one could take about the same length of time or more, putting us in the year 2015 to 2020, assuming the housing market bottoms out somewhere around 2008 or 2012. Homebuyers need to understand that these events do take place, and they need to be on the lookout for the signs in the housing marketplace before deciding whether or not to buy a home.

When Can I Lock In an Interest Rate, and Is It Feasible?

When? Whenever, and in whatever time period the lender will allow, and when the homebuyers are satisfied with the payment. However, homebuyers must remember that once they ask that the interest rate be locked in and the rates go down, you as homebuyers are committed to honoring your obligation to accept the locked-in interest rate that you agreed to accept, just as if the interest rates go up, in which case the lender becomes obligated to honor their lower quoted interest rate that has been locked in. So, the question still remaining is, is locking in an interest rate feasible? This is a question that can only be based upon the homebuyer's good judgment, the interest-rate market, and the homebuyers understanding of the mortgage loan market.

How to Compare Loans and Their Costs?

According to Regulation Z (the Truth in Lending Act), lenders are required to promote the informed use of consumer credit by requiring lenders to disclose credit terms in order to enable consumers to make comparisons between various lending sources. This act was implemented by the Board of Governors of the Federal Reserve System as a means to allow potential homebuyers the right and ability to compare lenders' rates and fees before deciding on which lender the homebuyers would like to use for their home loan. Therefore, all lenders are required by law to provide homebuyers with finance charges, as well as annual percentage rates (APRs) within a period of seventy-two hours after the loan application has been officially received and opened for processing by any lender. As the reader can now see, this process could get rather expensive if the homebuyers are into shopping their loan, because each lender you submit a loan application to will require all the previously mentioned fees up front as they have seventy-two hours after the loan application has been officially received and opened for processing before they are required to provide the homebuyers with this information. Nonetheless, the most confusing aspect of Regulation Z concerning the homebuyers is the quoted APR. The following explanation can become a little confusing for homebuyers to understand, but stay with me on this one, and if you have to re-read this section a few times to understand it, it will be well worth the effort.

Homebuyers viewing all the costs and fees showing in The Truth In Lending Act are usually pretty much self-explanatory until they view the quoted APR, at which time questions start flying from the homebuyers because they don't understand why there is a difference between the interest rate they were quoted and the interest rate shown as the APR. Likewise, the answers are normally inadequate as the majority of mortgage consultants and loan officers don't have the slightest idea of how to explain the APR, let alone the inner workings of the APR. At this point in time, absurdity starts running rampant, confusion sets in, and until the mortgage consultants or loan officers manage to come up with something that sounds feasible and acceptable to the homebuyer, nothing is accomplished. And even then, the acceptable answer that sounds sensible to the homebuyers will also be the wrong answer the majority of the time. Okay, let's untangle the confusion and understand how the APR works and why the APR is different from the quoted interest rate. If you happen to be a mortgage loan consultant or loan officer, you need to pay particular attention to this information so that you will be able to explain the ins and outs of the APR in your next encounter with homebuyers.

As everyone will note, there will be a variance between the finance charge or loan interest rate that the homebuyers have agreed to, that includes the APR. Nevertheless, the APR is the *"True Cost of Credit"* for a fully amortized loan over a period of fifteen, twenty, or thirty years, and assuming that you will live in your home for the entire duration of fifteen, twenty, or thirty years. The reason for the difference between the finance charge and the APR is based upon the final loan calculations, which are calculated over the full term of the loan. In other words, if the homebuyers decided to stay in their home for the entire duration of their loan, then the homebuyers would be subject to paying the total cost of the indicated APR, as this is the true cost of the loan according to the full amortization. On the other hand, if the homebuyers decide not to live in their home for the duration of the loan term, then homebuyers would not be subject to paying the quoted APR interest rate, but rather the interest rate that the loan was originally based upon as quoted by the lender.

In order to calculate the APR, lenders take the loan amount and subtract the nonrecurring closing costs. Then the lenders will find the interest rate that would correspond to the same payment factor as would be created by the total loan amount at the quoted interest rate minus the APR. Now, that's a mouthful, but I am going to break this down with an example so that everyone will be able to understand how the lenders establish the APR.

Example

Let's assume the homebuyers purchase a home for $330,000. Note: Regardless of what the dollar amount of the purchase price may be, the calculation of the APR will be the same. Let's also assume that the homebuyers made an initial investment, or down payment of $30,000 thereby financing $300,000. Now, let's assume the homebuyers were quoted a fixed interest rate of 10 percent for thirty years. We will now examine how the lenders go about establishing the annual percentage rate. The lenders take the homebuyer's loan amount of $300,000, and they subtract the homebuyer's nonrecurring closing costs, that include the broker and lender fees.

Now, let's assume the above fees are approximately $10,000. In addition to the homebuyer's initial investment of $30,000, he/ she will be required to pay for the nonrecurring closing costs, or, more to the point, the homebuyer will need approximately $40,000 in order to close the home loan transaction. Note: All nonrecurring closing costs will be tax deductible in the year they are paid on purchases, so be sure to keep a copy of the Regulation Z statement, as well as the good faith statement and the closing statement (HUD1) that will include the third-party fees discussed earlier. Okay, let's calculate the APR the same way the lenders will. First, take the loan amount of $300,000 quoted at 10 percent fully amortized for thirty years. This would give the homebuyer a monthly principal and interest payment of $2611.00 (rounded) per month. Now, let's deduct the nonrecurring costs of $10,000. We now have a figure of $290,000, even though the actual home loan will be for $300,000. This is the point where the lenders find the calculation that corresponds to the interest rate that would create the same payment factor that the total loan amount would create at the quoted percentage rate of 10 percent.

The lenders then calculate a percentage rate based on the $290,000 figure, which in this example would be approximately 10.4117%. This figure is known as the *"True Cost of Credit"*, the annual percentage rate, or the corresponding interest rate. The rate is created by calculating the total loan amount at the quoted interest rate minus the closing costs.

Assuming that you did not fully understand the above, please do not be discouraged, as 99.9 percent of all mortgage loan consultants, loan officers, and bankers do not know how to explain the annual percentage rate, let alone how it is calculated. However, if you take the time and read this section again or as many times as it may require, you will learn and understand how the banking institutions establish the APR, if you are so inclined. Furthermore, it should also be noted that different calculators will come up with different numbers when amortizing for the APR due to the different programming that goes into various calculators. In the above scenario I used a Hewlett-Packard 12C to arrive at the APR and when my wife used her Real Estate Master Qualifier Plus IIx, she came up with an APR of 10.307%. However, unless you are into amortizing and calculating APRs, I would suggest that homebuyers leave the final determination of the APR up to the banks.

What Are Points?

Point or *Points* are terms used in the lending industry to indicate dollar amounts, and are nothing more than percentage figures; e.g., 1 point equals 1 percent and 2 points equal 2 percent, etc. Points are usually calculated on the loan amount being financed and not on the actual purchase price of a home. Normally, points are fees paid to the lenders for originating, locating, and financing a home loan. The first point homebuyers pay normally goes to originating their mortgage loan. Additional points can be charged and used to buy the homebuyer's loan from a lender, which is known as the buy rate. Then, there are even more points that can be charged to homebuyers if they would like to buy down their interest rate; this is known as the buy-down rate, and can also be referred to as discount points, that are paid in addition to a commission to the lender as well as the mortgage loan consultant or loan officer. In other words, interest rates and points work on a teeter-totter principal, in that, if the homebuyers decide that they would like a lower interest rate for their home loan, then they will end up being charged more points in order for the lender to offset the cost to buy down a homebuyer's interest rate from a wholesale lender. Likewise, should a homebuyer decide to pay fewer points to fund a home loan, he/she would be quoted a higher interest rate because the lender would not be subjected to the higher cost to buy down the homebuyer's interest rate from the wholesale lender.

The above information can be a little confusing, so I will give you a brief overview of what was just stated. Let's say you purchase a home for $500,000 and want to finance $300.000 at 8 percent. If the lender decided to charge the homebuyers 1 point for buying the 8 percent interest rate and the mortgage loan consultant or loan officer charges an additional point to cover his/her commission, the homebuyer would end up paying a total of $6,000 to get the 8 percent interest rate. Now, let's say the homebuyers would like to have a 7 percent interest rate instead of the 8 percent rate they were quoted. The retail lender would call the wholesale lender and ask them what the additional buy-down rate would be in the form of points to get the homebuyer the 7 percent interest rate for their mortgage loan. In this situation, the wholesale lender tells the retail lender that the cost would be 1 point per ½-point reduction in the interest rate, or a total cost of 2 points in order to give the homebuyers the 7 percent interest rate. Now, based on the $300,000 being financed, the homebuyer would end up paying $12,000 in total points (2 points to the lender and 2 points for the buy-down rate) in order to get the 7 percent interest rate.

Nevertheless, before homebuyers make their decision to buy down the interest rate, they need to take into account two major considerations: (1) the payback period, and (2) the length of time they plan to live in their new home. Using the above financing figure of $300,000 as our example, let's look at the difference in financing at 8 percent vs. 7 percent in interest amortized over thirty years. At 8 percent the homebuyers would have a rounded monthly principal-and-interest payment of $2,187, and at 7 percent their rounded monthly principal-and-interest payment would be $1,984.00. Subtracting the $1,984.00 from the $2,187.00 yields a difference of $203 per month in savings using the 7 percent interest rate vs. the 8 percent interest rate. The homebuyers can now figure out the total time for the payback period, which would come to 59.11, months or 4.93 years, in order to get their $12,000 back by buying down the interest rate to 7 percent from 8 percent. However, if the homebuyers only plan on living in their home for five years or less, buying down the rate would not make much sense. On the other hand, if the homebuyers plan on living in their home for seven to ten years, then buying down the rate would continue to be to their advantage, and at the same time, the homebuyers would continue to benefit from the additional $203 per month in savings until they decided to sell their home.

Those in the lending industry also use what are known as rebate points. These are offered to the retail lenders by just about every wholesale lender in the loan market. This is a process whereby the mortgage loan consultant or loan officer quotes and charges zero points to homebuyers for their home loans. Now, you may be wondering how this can be possible, as the retail lenders and the mortgage loan consultants and loan officers have to make money in order to stay in business. Simple; the retail lenders get paid by the wholesale lenders in the form of rebate points. Here is how it works: The wholesale lenders decide that they want the retail lenders to sell a particular loan program to the homebuyers because this loan is a moneymaking loan for the wholesale lenders, but because the retail lenders are willing to sell any loan program to homebuyers, the wholesale lenders offer the retail lenders incentives in the form of rebate points to the mortgage loan consultants and loan officers so that they will sell particular mortgage loans to homebuyers.

In this situation, homebuyers need to be extremely careful that they fully understand the ins and outs of any given loan program that is being offered by the mortgage loan consultants and loan officers offering no-point loans or minimum-point loans, as these loan programs will generally not be your standard fixed-interest-rate loans. Nevertheless, let's say the wholesale lender is offering three rebate points to the mortgage loan consultants and loan officers for selling this particular loan program to homebuyers. What happens? The homebuyers get a no-point or no-cost loan, and the mortgage loan consultants or loan officers get three rebate points for selling this loan program. Now, based on the financing of $300,000, the retail lender is paid $9,000 in rebate points from the wholesale lender, and the homebuyers get their mortgage loans financed whether or not they fully understand the loan program they were given.

Furthermore, as far as the minimum-point loans go, in this scenario, the mortgage loan consultants or loan officers will usually show the unsuspecting homebuyers several different loan programs, giving homebuyers a minor explanation as to how these programs function, and then they will bring up the wholesale loan, offering the rebate points, and begin to attempt to extensively elaborate upon all the benefits that this particular loan program has to offer (whether or not they know anything about the inner workings of this loan program, which more than likely they don't), but they manage to make it sound great to the unsuspecting homebuyers who, unfortunately, fall for it hook, line, and sinker. And, as a super nice mortgage loan consultant or loan officer, they offer to charge the homebuyers only ½ a point for the loan. Wow! What a deal! The mortgage loan consultant or loan officer now knows that they will be making their company three points in the way of rebate points plus an additional ½ point for a total point cost of $10,500 based on the $300,000 in mortgage financing. The wholesale lenders will make a ton of money on this loan program because they will service or sell this loan immediately in the secondary market, as its yield will be greater than normal. Retail lenders also makes a lot of money for selling this loan program, and the unsuspecting homebuyers get a loan that they may or may not fully understand, but they will have their home loan or their refinanced loan monies.

Now let's look at how this process relates to and converts to a commission for the mortgage loan consultant or loan officer and his/her company. Mortgage loan consultants or loan officers working on a 50/50 point split, for example, charge a 1 percent buy rate in addition to a 1 percent loan origination fee for a total of 2 percent—1 percent paid to the wholesale lender and 1 percent paid to the retail lender. In this scenario, the wholesale lender gets 1 percent of $300,000, or $3,000, and the retail lender also gets 1 percent, or $3,000, which is split with the mortgage loan consultant or loan officer. Assuming the mortgage loan consultants or loan officers are working on a 50/50 point split with their company, they would make $1,500, and the company would also make $1,500.00.

Now, using our example above with the added benefit of receiving rebate points plus charging a ½ point in origination fees for a total of 3.50 percent, the wholesale lender gives the retail lender a check for the entire $10,500 dollars, and the retail lender then splits 50/50 with their mortgage loan consultants or loan officers, each making $5,250.00, and the wholesale lender, as I mentioned earlier, will make a considerable amount of money on this loan program as well.

Before moving on, there are a couple more things that homebuyers should know about, whether a homebuyer is buying a home or refinancing a home. The loan industry is limited by the amount of points that they are able to charge as wholesale and retail lenders, and according to the OTS, rebate points may not exceed four points maximum. The current formula for figuring the APR is based on the good faith statement, in which all of the non-recurring closing costs are tabulated and totaled and then multiplied by 5.99 percent, which is the maximum amount of points that can currently be charged by lenders without violating the Predatory Lending Law as established by the OTS.

Likewise, all rebates must be shown on both the initial good faith statement and the final good faith statement, and should the interest rate originally quoted change by an eighth of a point or more, and then an interim good faith statement must be issued to the homebuyers. Furthermore, without wholesale and retail lenders, mortgage loan consultants, and loan officers, nothing would happen in the housing marketplace. And yes, all of them are entitled to be paid, but remember, loan consultants, and loan officers get paid on the actual loan amount being financed, whereas real-estate agents and their real-estate companies get paid on the total sale price of a home. Nevertheless, just remember that all fees are negotiable in a real-estate or loan transaction.

What Is a Prepayment Penalty, and Do We Have to Accept It?

A prepayment penalty is a tool used by various lending institutions as a means of guaranteeing a lender that additional income will be received in the event that a homebuyer decides to sell his or her home before a given period of time has elapsed in homeownership. Because mortgage lenders are in the business of lending money and they believe that prospective homebuyers may be speculators or they have recently sold a home that they only lived in for two to three years or less, the lenders will be inclined to include a prepayment penalty clause in the loan documentation. Basically, the prepayment penalty clause will guarantee the lender that in the event that a homebuyer decides to sell a home in, say, three years or less, the lenders will be allowed to collect an additional six months of interest-only payments just because the homebuyer did not live in the home, for whatever reason, for a minimum of three years.

Homebuyers should understand that they are under no obligation whatsoever to accept a prepayment penalty clause in their loan documentation, as the end does not justify the means in this particular situation. In my professional opinion, there is absolutely no valid reason for any lender throughout the entire United States to require a prepayment penalty from homebuyers regardless of what the lender may be thinking at the time of granting a home loan. People buy and sell homes for a myriad of reasons, and to think that a lending institution has the right to coerce anyone it wants to agree to a prepayment penalty clause for whatever reason the lender may be thinking is outright ludicrous! Why should anyone be penalized for buying a home? Why should anyone be penalized for selling a home? Why should lenders be allowed to extort additional monies from their home-buying clients? To get free money; also known as

GREED!

Recently, there has been a new tactic being used by the lending institutions with regard to the prepayment penalty, and this is how it works. The lenders are offering to reduce the prospective homebuyer's interest rate by 1/8 percent to 1/25 percent below the prevailing market interest rate in order to entice the homebuyers into accepting a prepayment penalty clause. Furthermore, as an added incentive to the retail-selling lenders, the banks are offering them an additional rebate of 1 percent to 1.25 percent if they can talk their homebuyers into accepting a prepayment penalty. So who wins in this situation? Assuming a homebuyer stays in a home for thirty-seven months, the homebuyer will get the advantage of a reduced interest rate, the lender is guaranteed to collect a tremendous amount of interest, and the retail selling lender gets a bonus in the form of a rebate on the homeowner's loan amount. Therefore, in this particular situation we have what would be classified a perfect win-win-win situation in which everyone involved in the transaction benefits.

Why would anyone want to play by the lender's rules when it comes to a prepayment penalty? First of all, a prepayment penalty is exactly what it says—a penalty being assessed against homebuyers by lenders, forcing the homebuyers to live in their homes for a minimum of three years or be subjected to a penalty. Furthermore, the sub-prime lenders were giving homebuyers a three-year prepayment penalty on a two-year fixed loan thereby forcing the unsuspecting homebuyers into paying a higher percentage interest rate beginning in year three and forcing the homebuyers to pay as much as 12 percent or more in interest when their loans converted to the new mortgage loan terms with the same sub-prime rate lender. However, if the homebuyers decided to refinance their current loan before the expiration of the three-year prepayment period for a lower interest rate, then the homebuyers became subject to refinancing a larger mortgage loan by being forced to include the prepayment penalty that was still due and payable to the previous sub-prime lender. Talk about putting a loaded gun to the homebuyers head knowing full well that these lenders are not only ripping off the homebuyers, but they are also setting up these homebuyers for a foreclosure down the road. By being allowed to issue such a loan program to any homebuyer is not only ludicrous, but also an atrocity perpetrated on the unsuspecting homebuyers by these unscrupulous greedy and pernicious sub-prime lenders. Now you may understand why the housing market is in the situation that it is currently in throughout the United States. Nevertheless, as time goes on, hopefully, this situation will be addressed by the proper lending authorities including the OTS, or the OCC in order to see to it that this situation will never take place again in the United States. In my professional opinion, the use of a prepayment penalty by any mortgage lender throughout the United States should be against the law!

What Is Escrow, and Is It Required?

In simple terms, an escrow company is a third-party accumulation and distribution center. The common law definition, as stated in the Civil Code in California, states the following: "A grant may be deposited by the grantor with a third person, to be delivered on performance of a condition, and, on delivery by the depository, it will take effect. While in the possession of the third person and subject to conditions, it is called an Escrow." In other words, an escrow company accumulates and holds the funds and documents supplied by the sellers and buyers and makes concurrent delivery thereof, at the exact moment, when all of the terms and conditions of the home transaction have been performed.

Escrow companies function as distribution centers for the payments of all demands and as agencies that provide the clerical details in making pro-rations and adjustments for the settlements of accounts between transacting parties. Escrow companies are used to achieve a binding contract between the parties during the period of abeyance. In the state of California, independent escrow companies must be licensed and are regulated by the California Commissioner of Corporations. However, if a real-estate company maintains an escrow division, then that company would come under the jurisdiction of the Department of Real Estate in the state of California. Furthermore, depending on the regulations governing home transactions in the various other states throughout the United States, independent escrow companies may or may not be used, as some states will require the use of an attorney service to conduct these procedures. Nonetheless, I would advise homebuyers to check with their particular state concerning the governing body that would maintain jurisdiction over a home transaction in the event any problems should arise concerning the transaction.

Are Escrow Companies required? Yes and No. Allow me to explain. Escrows are required if there is a valid and enforceable contract between parties. This may concern real-estate sales and exchanges, the documenting of the loan transaction, the sale or encumbrance of personal property, sales or pledging of securities, sales of assets of a business, sales of promissory notes secured by trust deeds or mortgages, transfers of liquor licenses, or basically any transaction concerning a deed, bond, or other type of written obligation, delivered to a third person, to be delivered by him/her to the grantee only on the fulfillment of some condition. As anyone can now see, yes, escrows are required. Are independent escrow companies required? Based upon the above information, logic would indicate that escrow companies are indeed required. However, this is not entirely true, and I believe the general home-buying and refinancing public has the right to the truth, so here I go.

On the East Coast and in the Midwest, attorneys usually handle escrows. On the West Coast, title companies and independent escrow companies handle escrows. In California, as a rule, title companies handle escrows in Northern California and independent escrow companies handle escrows in Southern California. The advent of the independent escrow companies operating in Southern California amazes me for the simple reason that all title companies maintain escrow divisions within their companies and charge considerably less for their services than their counterparts, the independent escrow companies. However, it is understandable that this information is not widely known simply because the real-estate industry is not aware of this fact and the general home-buying and refinancing public has not been informed that they in fact have an alternative available to them when it comes to choosing an escrow company. Furthermore, the general home-buying and refinancing public has the right to request that the title company being used, also be allowed to do their escrow.

Remember, all real-estate fees are negotiable. As with title companies, anyone can negotiate fees with any escrow company, and to my amazement, I discovered that the majority of real-estate agents do not have the slightest idea that one can negotiate the fees with an escrow company. In fact, other than myself as a loan consultant, as well as a large number of mortgage loan consultants, loan officers, real-estate agents, and brokers that were trained at the Professional Loan Officer Training Center, I know of no other mortgage loan consultants, loan officers, real-estate agents or brokers (which also includes the majority of the mortgage lenders) who have the ability to negotiate escrow fees for their clients. It has been my experience that when I called an escrow company to "offer" the opportunity to do the escrow of a particular real-estate transaction, my decision to grant that company the transaction depended on the amount of escrow fee discounts they could offer to my clients.

As a loan consultant, I have always managed to save my clients a minimum of $250 on their escrow fees. Now, the way I viewed this savings from my perspective was, unless home sellers or home buyers could make $250 or more in five or ten minutes, then it would be to their advantage to have their real-estate agent or mortgage loan consultant or loan officer take the time to negotiate the escrow fees with the escrow companies. Caution: It is not uncommon for home sellers or home buyers or their real-estate agents to request a particular escrow company be used to handle their escrows. Homebuyers need to be careful here, as they can end up paying excessive fees for their escrow. However, I will show everyone how to handle this situation with the opposition at the end of the next section.

What Is Title Insurance, and Is It Required?

Title insurance not only protects the homebuyer's and seller's property, but it also protects them from others who may attempt to claim their property in the future. Is it required? Yes, but remember this: "No worthwhile investment is ever secured unless it is insured." Basically, a policy of title insurance insures the ownership of an estate or interest in land, or the priority and validity of an encumbrance on land or in an estate. Title insurance is a contract between the sellers or buyers and the title insurance company, to indemnify against loss through defects in the title or against liens or encumbrances that may affect the title at the time the policy is issued.

As with other kinds of insurance, different types of title insurance coverage are offered and available. The most widely used form of title insurance policy in California is the standard coverage policy, but an extended coverage policy is also available; the extended coverage policy insures against loss or damage from additional matters not included within the coverage of the standard title policy. Homebuyers should also understand that they have the right to request that the sellers pay for an extended title insurance policy when purchasing a home. In the event the sellers disagree with the homebuyers' request, then the homebuyers should ask their mortgage lender to inform them of what the additional cost would be for a title insurance extended policy. Remember, neither title policy will provide complete and full coverage, but the protection of an extended policy will afford invaluable protection to homebuyers. And, the additional cost for the extended policy vs. the standard coverage policy will be minimal compared with the additional protection the extended policy will offer to the homebuyers.

Nevertheless, when homebuyers are purchasing real property in the state of California, they will be required to indicate how they will be taking title to the property for the necessity of the recording laws. Therefore, unless homebuyers are taking title as a single person in severalty, they may want to seek legal advice from an attorney in order to receive the legal explanations and understandings as to how they should or would like to take or indicate the form of title vesting they desire. Currently, in California, the available forms of title vesting are tenancy in common, joint tenancy, community property, and tenancy in partnership. Likewise, California is classified as a community property state, so be sure to talk to an attorney as well as an accountant if you intend to purchase land in California, as there are various advantages and disadvantages to the different ways of taking title to property, as well as advantages and disadvantages concerning the IRS and the State of California's tax laws.

Here is another priceless piece of information homebuyers should be made aware of: They have the right to negotiate their title fees with any title company through their mortgage loan consultant, loan officer or real-estate agent. In fact, homebuyers should ask their mortgage loan consultant, loan officer or real-estate agent to give them not less than three title fee quotes. Pay attention, because this information is not only important, but it is also little known within the real-estate industry that one has the right to negotiate title fees.

As I indicated at the end of the previous section, I am now going to show everyone how to handle home sellers or homebuyers or real-estate agents who want to request the use of a particular escrow company to handle their escrow or a combination of both an escrow and title insurance company.

Because it is extremely important for homebuyers to understand, I am going to point out once again that, firstly, everything, including every fee, is negotiable in a real-estate transaction. Secondly, in the event that the seller's real-estate agent and/or the seller insists on a particular escrow and/or title company to be used, then the homebuyer has the right to insist that in the event that they can find an escrow and/or title company that will charge them less money for their escrow and/or title insurance fees, the seller will agree to pay the difference in the escrow and/or title insurance fees for insisting that the homebuyers use the seller's escrow and/or title company. Likewise, homebuyers can also request that the selling real-estate agent pay for any excess title insurance fees out of his/her own commission in the event that the selling real-estate agent insists that the homebuyers use a particular escrow and/or title company by indicating said escrow and/or title company in the written real estate contract, and this should be done by the homebuyer's agent in a written counteroffer to the sellers.

Thirdly, sellers can insist that their real-estate agent be required to pay for any excess escrow and/or title fees on behalf of the homebuyers, as well as any excess escrow and/or title fees that the sellers may be required to pay in the event that the selling real-estate agent insist that all parties to the real-estate transaction be required to use the selling real-estate agent's recommendation for indicating any particular escrow and/or title company! Because everything in a real-estate transaction is negotiable, it would be wise for not only the sellers, but also the homebuyers, to check with not less than three different escrow and title companies to make a comparison of their fees.

As was stated in the previous section, everyone can negotiate with title companies concerning their fees! Likewise, and again as was previously mentioned, very few real-estate agents, mortgage loan consultants, and loan officers realize that title insurance fees can be negotiated. Furthermore, I have saved my clients a minimum of $250 on their title insurance fees. I now believe that homebuyers are starting to realize that they can save a considerable amount of money simply by questioning real-estate transaction fees and negotiating for lower fees.

Think about this for a moment: Why would anyone want to use an independent escrow company and a separate title company for their home transaction? If you remember, I indicated earlier that all title companies maintain in-house escrow divisions. So why use separate companies for the same transaction? It is simply a matter of requesting that whatever title company is used will also handle the escrow transaction. Likewise, there are major advantages to using a title company's in-house escrow division to handle the same real-estate transaction. For example, far fewer transaction fees can be requested and negotiated in such a case because the title company is getting both the escrow and title fees; therefore, the fees can be considerably less. Simply have the mortgage loan consultant, loan officer, or real-estate agent inform the title company that they are willing to give the title business to them along with the escrow transaction, assuming that they are willing to cut their fees by, say, 15 to 25 percent. Will they do it? Sure they will, because they want the business.

Another great advantage of using the title company's in-house escrow division comes about in the event that something is wrong with the title on the property in question. This could be a clouded title problem or simply a cloud on the title that needs to be identified and corrected in order to proceed with the escrow closing. Now, if the homebuyers are using an independent escrow company and this situation arises, the escrow company has to call the title company and make a request for verification, clarification, and removal of any clouds affecting the title before proceeding with the escrow instructions. This process could take two weeks or more before it is resolved and the independent escrow company is notified that they can proceed with the escrow.

As a professional loan consultant, I had this happen to my loan transactions a number of times before I got the message and started using the title company's in-house escrow division. Why? Because, in this situation it was just simply a matter of the in-house escrow division notifying the title company (usually located in the same facility) of the problem and within a matter of a few hours or so the problem was resolved without interrupting the flow of documentation through the title company's escrow division. Nevertheless, I learned this the hard way, and from then on I always used the title company's in-house escrow division. Likewise, I used to do the negotiating with the title companies and their escrow divisions automatically for all of the clients I did loan transactions for over the several years I worked as a loan consultant, and not once was I ever denied these discounts from the title companies for using their in-house escrow divisions. Homebuyers, feel free to request, indicate, or demand that a particular title company and their in-house escrow division be used for your home purchase and home loan transaction. And if the homebuyer is turned down, then be sure to inform the seller, the real-estate agent, or the suggesting party that he/she will have to pay for any difference should escrow or title fees be more than what the homebuyer can get through his/her recommendations as long as it is part of the purchase contract. Homebuyers, be sure to get escrow and title insurance fee quotes in writing so you can submit them to the seller, real-estate agent, or suggesting party for reimbursement.

What Is PMI, MIP, and VA Insurance?

PMI stands for Private Mortgage Insurance and applies to conventional mortgage loans. Homebuyers may also hear the term MI, which stands for Mortgage Insurance, but this is essentially the same as PMI. MIP stands for Mortgage Insurance Premium and applies to FHA mortgage loans, and the VA also maintains a high-risk insurance that is incorporated into the VA funding fee.

These are insurance companies that specialize in high-risk mortgage insurance coverage, which is normally required by lenders who are willing to underwrite and finance homebuyers who maintain loan-to-value (LTV) ratios that are greater than 80 percent. In other words, the homebuyers who do not have the ability to make a full 20 percent down payment are placed in the lender's high-risk classification. Likewise, these additional insurance premium requirements are designed to protect the lenders in the event of a default on behalf of the homebuyers. The greater the LTV that the homebuyers have, the more the monthly insurance premium will cost the homebuyers, because of the greater risk that the lenders assume with these types of mortgage loans. As it currently stands, the lending industry allows homebuyers to include the PMI, MIP, and VA high risk insurance premiums to be included in the home loan financing.

Is It a Requirement to Have Private Mortgage Insurance (PMI)?

Yes and No. It all depends on the LTV that the homebuyers have on the property they intend to purchase. If the homebuyers intend to put 5, 10, 15, or even 19 percent down as their down payment, then yes, the lenders will require private mortgage insurance in order to protect their investment in the event the homebuyers default on their mortgage loan. On the other hand, if the homebuyers put 20 percent or more down, then, no, they will not be required to purchase private mortgage insurance. Homebuyers should also know that in the event the lender requires private mortgage insurance, they can finance the entire premium into their mortgage loan, thereby eliminating any further out-of-pocket expenses. In addition, because the mortgage insurance premium is added into the mortgage loan, homebuyers will be able to write off the interest on their federal taxes. Moreover, the homebuyers must be sure to request a breakdown of said interest from their escrow company. This information is also reflected on the IRS 1098 form, which is received each year from the lender.

Is It a Requirement to Always Have to Pay PMI, MIP, and VA Insurance?

Yes and No. According to the underwriting guidelines of FNMA and FHLMC, they have relaxed their policies on the cancellation of PMI when the equity in the homebuyer's home reaches twenty percent or more. Therefore, homebuyers can now request that their the PMI be canceled after two years if scheduled principal payments plus any prepayment of the principal increases the homebuyers' home equity by 20 percent or more. Furthermore, PMI may also be canceled after two years if additions to the home or home improvements have increased the equity ratio to 20 percent or more. However, homebuyers must wait five years if they count only on home appreciation to raise their equity ratio to 20 percent or more. Nonetheless, the cancellation of PMI can be requested by the homebuyers when their home appreciates 25 percent or more within two to five years by notifying the mortgage lender, who will verify said appreciation with the insurance company providing the PMI mortgage insurance.

Nevertheless, in all situations, homebuyers must petition the lender to cancel their PMI. Furthermore, homebuyers must not have been more than sixteen to twenty days late on their mortgage installment payments more than once during the past twelve months or more than thirty days past due any one time during the preceding twelve months. And, if a homebuyer's mortgage loan has an adjustable rate or a graduated payment schedule, one year must have passed since the last increase in the monthly mortgage installment of principal and interest. Finally, homebuyers must pay for an appraisal to document that their equity has reached the specified value. Likewise, failure to follow any of these criteria for canceling PMI will allow the lenders to continue charging homebuyers PMI indefinitely.

Let's now address the question as to whether or not MIP and VA high-risk insurance premiums can be eliminated. The answer is yes, this is possible, but highly unlikely. The reason that MIP and VA high-risk insurance is unlikely to be eliminated is that government mortgage loans usually maintain very high loan balances, making them extremely high-risk loans for the government-approved lenders. The possibility of a homebuyer's equity increasing in value to a point where that homebuyer's home equity is 20 percent or greater within five years or less may be slim to none. Again, this will depend on exactly how much of a down payment the homebuyer made as well as the LTV established at the time that the mortgage loan was financed.

Because both MIP and VA high-risk insurance will normally be required by an approved government lender, attempting to eliminate this insurance will require homebuyers to seek an attorney or a specialist who understands the government's requirements, as well as the insurance underwriting guidelines that would allow the homebuyers to eliminate this high risk insurance. As the reader can now see, the chances of eliminating MIP or VA insurance requirements are not only slim, but the cost factor that may be involved would not be sufficient enough for the homebuyers to recoup the monetary expenditure that would be required to offset the MIP or VA high-risk insurance. Furthermore, it should be pointed out that the Federal Housing Authority (FHA) requires the MIP stay on the loan for the life of the loan. Likewise, the current insurance premiums for MIP average $50 per month per $100,000 financed, and PMI averages $100 per month per $100,000 financed, and again, PMI can be removed.

SECTION 3: PARTS OF A LOAN AND LOAN COMPARISONS

What Is a Margin or Spread?

Before I get started with this section, I would like to point out some standard terminology that is used in the lending industry so that the homebuyers will become familiar with these terms as I continue to proceed with the discussion of the various mortgage loan programs that are being offered and used in the home marketplace.

Starting with the above caption, the words margin and spread maintain the same meaning and are nothing more than interchangeable terminology being used by the lending institutions when they are talking about the adjustable-interest-rate loans. Note: For the sake of simplicity, I will be using the term "margin" as opposed to "margin and spread" throughout the remainder of the text. However, it should be noted that the margin serves three distinct functions concerning the adjustable-interest-rate loans, which are as follows: (1) the margin is the fixed aspect of the adjustable-interest-rate loan, (2) the margin is also the built-in profit to the lenders who decide to service these loans during the first five-year viability period of the adjustable-interest-rate loan, and (3) the greater the margin, the greater the yield, and hence the easier it is to sell the loan in the secondary market. Note: All loans are eventually sold to the secondary market, and unless the lender decides to continue servicing the homebuyer's mortgage loan, as opposed to selling the loan in the secondary market after the five-year viability period, then the lender will continue to profit from the loan as the lender makes between .250 percent and .375 percent from the margin in the form of servicing fees for as long as they continue to service the loan.

Because the adjustable-interest-rate loans are extremely complex and technical, I will only point out at this time, that it is vital for the homebuyers to ask for, select, or buy down the margin as low as possible, e.g., 2.25, 2.50, 2.75, etc., when they are seeking or accepting an adjustable-interest-rate loan. In other words, when the margin is added to the index that the loan has been tied to, the lower the margin, the lower the overall interest rate will be throughout the duration of the adjustable-interest-rate loan, and the less profit the lenders will be able to continue to make on the homebuyer's loan. Furthermore, margins that are in excess of 3.00 percent or 3.50 percent are not only excessive, but they will continue to cost the homebuyers additional monies throughout the term of the adjustable-interest-rate loan. Homebuyers should also know that the lenders make a considerable amount of monies on mortgage loans they fund and service, as well as even more monies when they sell these loans in the secondary market. Therefore, in my opinion, excessive margins being offered to the home-buying public should be regulated by the OTS or OCC to assure homebuyers a fair, honest, and reasonable home loan transaction in exchange for accepting an adjustable-interest-rate loan program.

Nevertheless, it is important for homebuyers to realize that they have the right to negotiate the margin with their lender. However, even though very few homebuyers know, realize or understand that they can negotiate the margin with a lender, they need to understand that it can become extremely expensive to buy down a margin simply because they are reducing the profit structure to the lender. Likewise, because the inner workings of all adjustable-interest-rate loans are extremely complex in their makeup, and extremely complicated to understand, it is my recommendation that all homebuyers seek out an expert who knows and understands the adjustable-interest-rate mortgage loan, and one who can explain, or better yet, graph out, and at the same time, explain the adjustable-interest-rate loan program to the prospective homebuyers until they have a full and complete understanding of the inner workings of an adjustable loan program.

What Is a Loan Cap?

When referring to a loan cap in the lending industry in relation to an adjustable-interest-rate loan program can become very confusing, as the term loan cap is being used in the adjustable-interest-rate loan industry to describe four separate and distinct categories that are all connected in one way or another that makes up the adjustable-interest-rate loan. Therefore, I will attempt to give the homebuyers a breakdown and an understanding of the four areas in the adjustable loan programs where lenders use this term interchangeably with or without fully understanding what they are talking about or referring to in the adjustable loan, thereby creating mass confusion on behalf of the prospective homebuyers. Because of this confusion, I will view each one of the four loan cap categories separately in an attempt to explain the advantages and disadvantages that may apply to the terminology of a loan cap, and they are as follows: (1) The adjustable-interest-rate loan cap, (2) The annual payment loan cap, (3) The maximum life or ceiling of the loan cap, and (4) The maximum add-on or wrap-around of any deferred interest the loan may become subjected to, also known as a loan cap.

Viewing #1:

This is an adjustable-interest-rate loan cap that applies only to the no-negative, or payment-shock loan, and will limit the amount of the interest rate payment increases that could occur in this loan depending on whether the loan maintains a semiannual or annual adjustable–interest-rate loan cap. In other words, does the loan maintain a 1 percent interest rate loan cap once every six months, or does the loan maintain a 2 percent annual interest rate loan cap? In the event that the homebuyer's loan fits this scenario, then this is a no-negative, or payment-shock loan. In other words, the 1 percent interest rate loan cap means that this loan payment will increase 10 percent once every six months until the loan reaches the current interest rate market level. Likewise, the 2 percent annual interest rate loan cap means that this loan rate cap will increase 20 percent at the end of the first year, and will continue to increase again until it reached the current equivalent market interest rate level. Also, as long as there are any fluctuations in the interest rate market, this loan will continue to adjust to keep pace with the interest rates as this loan cannot become subjected the deferred interest. It should also be noted that the 2 percent annual rate increase adjustable loan is going to the wayside, as the 1 percent semiannual increases seem to be more desirable to the lending institutions as they do not have to wait as long for the loan to start increasing, and catching up with the current interest market.

Viewing #2:

This is an adjustable payment cap loan that has a built-in protector that will limit the amount of increases in the monthly mortgage payments on an annual basis and applies to the negative, or option loan, and the graduated-payment mortgage loan. This loan is normally limited to a 7.50 percent payment cap, and as a rule, a possible negative amortization or a deferred adjustable-interest-rate loan. As an example, comparing #1 and #2, let's assume a $1000 monthly mortgage payment subject to a 1 percent semiannual or 2 percent annual payment loan cap adjustment. At the end of the homebuyer's first year's monthly mortgage payments, the payments would reflect a 20 percent increase having a 2 percent annual adjustment increase, or a $1,200 monthly mortgage payment in year two. Whereas, the same $1,000 monthly mortgage payment having a 7.50 percent annual payment loan cap adjustment could not exceed $1,075 in the monthly mortgage payment in year two.

I realize that this can be a little confusing to homebuyers, but feel free to review "What Are Negative Loans, and Are They Beneficial?" before you make or commit to making an adjustable-interest-rate loan decision. Remember, if you have a payment loan cap adjustment and the current monthly mortgage payment is $1,000, this loan will limit the increased annual monthly mortgage loan payment to only 7.50 percent or $1,075 in year two. However, in the event that the homebuyers have a no negative, or payment shock loan, their monthly mortgage loan payment will increase to $1,200 or more in twelve months in order to fully amortize their loan according to the note interest rate, because this loan is not subject to deferred interest. Homebuyers, be careful with adjustable-interest-rate loan caps as opposed to adjustable-interest-rate payment loan caps.

Viewing #3:

The life cap (L/C), also known as the life of the loan cap of an adjustable-interest-rate loan, is technically the maximum interest rate a homebuyer could become subject to in the form of a maximum monthly mortgage payment at anytime over the life of the loan. In other words, in the event of run away inflation, like that which occurred in 1982, the adjustable-interest-rate loan could never exceed the quoted L/C regardless of what inflation may do concerning interest rates. The L/C limits the maximum interest rate (10%, 11%, 12%, etc.) that the monthly mortgage loan payment could become subjected to throughout the entire duration of the loan. Moreover, it is extremely important for homebuyers to understand that the L/C and the margin as they are considered to be the most important aspects of any adjustable loan, depending upon how long the homebuyers intend to live in their home, as well as the current economic conditions concerning the interest-rate market.

Viewing #4:

The use of the term loan cap, as used here, concerns the maximum amount of deferred interest that would be allowed to accumulate, and be added on to the original loan amount financed at the time the adjustable-interest-rate loan becomes eligible for recasting or re-amortization three, five, or more years after the loan has been in effect. This would only occur in, and affect adjustable-interest-rate loans that are subject to deferred interest, and this includes the negative, or option, loan and the graduated payment mortgage loan. Likewise, as stated previously, this is also referred to as a wraparound loan concerning deferred interest, a term used mostly on the West Coast, whereas the term loan cap is used on the East Coast.

Caution: Even though both the no negative and the payment shock loan, and the negative, or option loan, must maintain L/Cs according to the federal government, homebuyers need to be made aware of the fact that some federal savings-and-loan banking institutions were attempting to incorporate an adjustable-interest-rate life cap into the homebuyers' adjustable-interest-rate loans. In other words, the federal savings-and-loan banking institutions were quoting homebuyers an initial L/C that was to remain in effect for only the first five years of their loan, and then these lenders were attempting to increase the homebuyers' L/C anywhere from 2 percent to 2.5 percent over the homebuyers' existing L/C, that was to remain in effect throughout the remaining duration of the homebuyers' loans. In my opinion, not only is this process ridiculous, but it is also ludicrous to think that these lenders were attempting to play psychics by endeavoring to forecast some unknown future event that may or may not take place in the mortgage loan interest-rate market, all to the determent of the unsuspecting homebuyers. After all, if the lenders want to play psychics, then they should also offer the homebuyers the option of reducing their L/C from 2 to 2.5 percent downward if the lenders think that something will change in the future concerning what may or may not happen in the mortgage loan interest-rate market.

As previously stated, the most important aspect for homebuyers to consider when applying for an adjustable-interest-rate loan is obtaining the lowest possible margin, preferably 3 percent or less, and the life cap, preferably not more than 6 percent over the start rate. Therefore, it becomes extremely important for homebuyers to question a lender as to any so-called automatic adjustable-interest-rate life cap that can affect the overall amortization of the adjustable-interest-rate loan. Furthermore, as to the legality of this recent inception of an adjustable-interest-rate life cap being allowed to be incorporated by the federal savings-and-loan banking institutions, this matter, as of this writing, has not been addressed by the OTS or the OCC for their evaluation and determination as to whether or not this process is legal according to Regulation Z, and the truth-in-lending laws. Nonetheless, even though this practice was quite prevalent in the early and mid-1990s, I have not heard about this situation occurring in recent years. However, until this issue has been addressed by the appropriate government agencies, it is my recommendation and suggestion that homebuyers do not accept any so-called adjustable-interest-rate loans that maintain an adjustable-interest-rate life cap clause or rider in the loan documentation!

Start Rate vs. Margin vs. Note Rate vs. Index vs. Payment Cap or Interest-Rate Loan Cap VS Life Cap

Yes, this is a mouthful, but it is extremely important to understand should homebuyers be inclined to seek an adjustable-interest-rate loan. However, before I get started, I would like to outline the standard format of the adjustable-interest-rate loan, and give the homeowners and the prospective homebuyers a brief explanation concerning the terms associated with the adjustable-interest-rate loan, which follows:

Start Rate	Margin or Spread	Note Rate	Index	Pmt. Cap or Int. Rate Loan Cap	Life Cap

The start rate is the initial interest rate at which the initial monthly mortgage payment will be calculated. This is also referred to as the minimum monthly mortgage payment.

The margin is the fixed aspect of the adjustable-interest-rate loan, and it will remain fixed throughout the duration of the loan as the margin is also part of the additional profit in the loan to lenders.

The note rate is the effective interest rate, and monthly mortgage payment that homebuyers should be making on their adjustable-interest-rate loan. This factor alone gives the negative loan its other name—option loan—because it gives the homebuyers the option to determine which monthly mortgage payment they would like to make, e.g., the start rate payment, interest only payment, or the note rate payment. This will be explained in much greater detail when the readers view the section outlining and explaining the sixteen major advantages the adjustable negative loan has to offer the homebuyers.

The index is the variable, or fluctuating aspect of the adjustable-interest-rate loan. By taking the fixed figure in the margin and adding it to the variable figure indicated in the index, anyone can establish the effective note rate. For example: the margin equals 2.50 percent and the index is 5.25 percent. By adding these two figures together the homebuyers can get an effective note rate, or interest rate of 7.75 percent or the interest rate payment that the note rate is calculated on, in order to establish the monthly mortgage principal-and-interest payment that the homebuyers should be making in order to avoid the accumulation of any deferred interest, that would be added back to the original loan amount thereby increasing the loan balance.

The payment cap and interest rate loan cap are the built-in loan adjustment protectors that are designed to limit the amount of monthly or annual payment increases homebuyers could become subjected to over a stated period of time, e.g., fifteen, twenty, or thirty years.

The life cap is the maximum interest rate that homebuyers could become subjected to throughout the entire duration of the adjustable-interest-rate loan.

Now that I have given homeowners and homebuyers a brief explanation, and the standard format of an adjustable-interest-rate loan, let's now view some important questions that anyone buying a home should ask his/her mortgage loan consultant, loan officer, or lender with regard to any adjustable-interest-rate loan programs.

Question: Is the life cap tied to the start rate or the note rate? Example: Let's say the homebuyers have a start rate of 3.875 percent and a note rate of 6.625 percent, and the lender is going to apply a 6.000 percent add-on in order to establish a life cap. Is the lender going to apply the add-on to the start rate of 3.875 percent that would give the homebuyers an effective life cap interest rate of 9.875 percent? Or is the lender going to apply the add-on to the note rate of 6.625 percent that would give the homebuyers an effective life cap of 12.625 percent? Now the homebuyers can see why it is so important to understand the inner workings of an adjustable-interest-rate loan, and why they should negotiate for the lowest possible life cap, making sure that the lender is applying any add-on interest rate to the start rate and not the note rate.

Incidentally, the current add-on interest rate percentage figures being utilized by the federal savings-and-loan banking institutions in establishing the life caps, range from 5 percent to 6 percent, and are usually applied to the start rates, assuming that the homebuyers are dealing with a reputable lending institution as opposed to prevaricating varlets, and also assuming that the start rates are not in the .500 percent or .750 percent start ranges. Furthermore, it is important for the homebuyers to understand that the higher the Start Rates are, the better the odds are for getting the life cap add-on applied to the start rates. Remember, the lenders are in the business of making money, and the greater the difference between the start rates and the note rates, the more money the lenders will make. Likewise, the lower the start rates are, the less sense it would make for the lenders to add on their percentage to a rate that would be lower than, or equivalent to the note rates, as this would limit and delay the lenders from making profit on their the loans.

Are Fixed Rates More Expensive Than Adjustable Rates?

They used to be; however, it depends on the financial market and the economic transition period that we are in or are approaching. Normally, adjustable interest rate mortgages (ARM's) are less expensive in the first few years of the loan. However, in today's financial market, adjustable-interest-rate loans may or may not make any sense depending on where the current fixed-interest-rate market is at the time homebuyers apply for a home loan.

When the fixed-interest-rate market on a thirty-year loan is approximately 8.500% to 10.500%, adjustable loans can offer the homebuyers major advantages. In a high-fixed-interest-rate market, the adjustable-interest-rate loans will normally have a much lower starter interest rate, which will reflect a lower monthly mortgage loan payment than the homebuyers could obtain with a fixed-interest-rate loan. Furthermore, homebuyers would also be able to qualify for more property at a higher dollar amount than they could normally qualify for with a fixed-interest-rate loan, because they would be qualifying at interest rates one or two percentage points less, depending on the current interest-rate market conditions. Likewise, most adjustable-interest-rate lenders will be qualifying prospective homebuyers on their mortgage loan simply based on the margin plus the current index of the adjustable-interest-rate loan, known as the note rate, but allowing the homebuyers the option of making considerably lower payments based on the start rate.

Before going any further, I need to point out that it is mandatory that prospective homebuyers receive an in-depth explanation of any adjustable loan they may be considering, and a complete understanding as to how these adjustable loans work from a thoroughly knowledgeable mortgage loan consultant, loan officer, or lender, as homebuyers could end up in serious trouble without the knowledge and understanding of how adjustable loans work. In the mortgage loan industry, homebuyers may be able to find at least one thoroughly knowledgeable mortgage loan consultant, loan officer, or lender who understands the inner workings of the adjustable loan programs out of every ten or more lenders. However, the further away homebuyers are from any major metropolitan area, the poorer the odds of finding a thoroughly knowledgeable mortgage loan consultant, loan officer, or lender. The odds may be one in one hundred or more, so it is extremely important for homebuyers being offered adjustable-interest-rate loan programs to seek out that one exceptional and thoroughly knowledgeable mortgage loan consultant, loan officer, or lender who can best educate them on the inner workings of the adjustable loan. Take a trip to the nearest major city in your area and try to locate a thoroughly knowledgeable mortgage loan consultant, loan officer, or lender, as it will be well worth your time.

Technically, there are only two adjustable-interest-rate loans in the mortgage-loan market throughout the entire United States, even though the loan industry has a ton of acronyms that relate to these adjustable loan programs. Furthermore, and non-technically, there is also another loan that has been used by the lending industry on and off over the years known as a graduated-payment mortgage loan that functions like an adjustable-interest-rate loan, but in fact, it is also classified as a fixed-rate loan, that I will also be covering in this section. Moreover, in my personal opinion, all of the adjustable loan acronyms which have been concocted by the lending industry over the years have been designed to accomplish only two things: (1) to confuse the heck out of the mortgage loan consultants, loan officers and lenders, and (2) to confuse the heck out of the general home-buying public. Nevertheless, these adjustable-interest-rate loan programs are known as the no-negative loan, AKA the payment shock loan; the negative loan, AKA the option loan; and the graduated-payment mortgage loan, AKA the semi-boneless ham loan. However, at the present time the negative adjustable loan has not emerged back into the mortgage loan marketplace.

Let's briefly go over these adjustable loan programs in order to give the prospective homebuyers a basic understanding of how these loans function, and keep in mind that all of these mortgage loans maintain the same common denominator, in that all of them will allow the homebuyers to qualify and purchase more property because homebuyers will be qualifying at lower interest rates than they could qualify for at the current fixed-interest-rate market, assuming that we are in or are approaching an interest-rate market of 8 percent, 9 percent, 10 percent or higher like they used to be back in the late '70s and '80s. Incidentally, for those of you who do not remember this period of time, it was considered to be a healthy economy when the interest rates in the mortgage loan market were running in the 8%-to-10% range.

Starting with the no-negative loan, this is an adjustable loan that maintains the standard adjustable loan format (that I will be covering further on in this book), in that this loan has a start rate, margin, note rate, index, loan cap and a life cap (L/C). To identify this adjustable loan as a no-negative loan, the loan will indicate a 1 percent increase in six months or a 2 percent annual increase, that this mortgage loan may become subjected to in any given twelve-month period of time. However, because this adjustable loan is not subject to any deferred interest, the lenders must continue to increase the monthly mortgage loan payment by 1 percent (six months) or 2 percent (annually) until the monthly mortgage loan payment reaches the established note rate of the homebuyer's mortgage loan. Furthermore, in a runaway interest-rate market, the lenders will continue to increase the monthly mortgage loan payment until it reaches the life cap as we have previously discussed.

Let's incorporate some numbers in this loan, and look at an example of how the no-negative loan, AKA the payment shock loan functions. Let's assume a homebuyer purchased a home for $500,000 and is financing $250,000, and will be using one of the no-negative adjustable loans (adjusting at 1 percent every six months or 2 percent maximum annually), currently on the market having a Start Rate of 6.75 Percent, a margin of 3.00 percent, an index of 4.99 percent, and an effective note rate of 7.99 percent (that is found by adding the margin to the index figure). Now remember, the lenders are not in the business of subsidizing homebuyers' loans, so is what will happen to this loan, and the homebuyer's monthly mortgage payments using the Real Estate Master Qualifier Plus IIIx calculator. Taking the $250,000 in financing and amortizing the loan for thirty years using the note rate payment, we arrive at a monthly required loan payment of $1,833.00 (rounded) for a principal-and-interest payment. However, the homebuyer is starting the monthly mortgage payments based on the start rate of 6.75 percent, thereby paying only $1,622.00 (rounded) on the principal and interest.

Do the homebuyers think that they will incur the 1 percent monthly mortgage loan payment increase at the end of the first sixth month of this loan? Most definitely, because the lender is eating the difference in the interest rate until they are able to get the monthly mortgage loan payment up to the current note rate payment. Therefore, the lender adds 1 percent to the start rate payment, and assuming nothing has changed in the way of the index being used, the homebuyer's new monthly mortgage payment will be $1,791.00 (rounded) based on the new adjusted start rate of 6.75 percent plus the 1 percent increase, that equals 7.75 percent in the form of the new monthly interest, or an increase of $170.00 (rounded) in the principal-and-interest payment, or just a little over a 10 percent increase in the first six months of the monthly mortgage payment.

Now remember, the homebuyer has still not reached the current note rate of 7.99 percent, nor is he/she making monthly payments of $1,833.00 (rounded) as required by the no-negative loan. Therefore, the homebuyer will take another increase in their monthly mortgage loan payment again in the next six months in order to reach the required $1,833.00 (rounded) monthly principal-and-interest payment. Now is the time when this particular no-negative loan can become scary and dangerous, especially, if the homebuyers were not fully informed as to the inner workings of this loan. Let's look at both scenarios. In the first scenario, the homebuyers are hoping that their index does not increase and is relatively stable, which in turn will keep their monthly mortgage payment consistent. On the other hand, the lenders realize that the monthly indexes are constantly changing with the interest-rate market and are hoping that the index rate goes up so that they can make more money on the adjustable no-negative loan. Furthermore, homebuyers should understand that the loan terms of 1 percent every 6 months or 2 percent annually will remain in effect throughout the term of this loan or until such a time that the homebuyers realize their mistake, and refinance out of the adjustable no-negative loan.

Homebuyers should now be able to understand why the no-negative loan is referred to as the payment shock loan. Likewise, the no-negative loan will normally place the homebuyer's monthly mortgage payment over the fixed rate market within three to five years or in less time depending on the difference between the start rate and the note rate. In addition, homebuyers may be faced with long-term interest rates as high as 11.750 percent or 12.990 percent (using the above scenario, and depending on whether the lender adds five points to the start rate or the note rate), or more depending on the structure of a lender's particular adjustable loan and their L/C. In other words, in a volatile interest-rate market, assuming that the homebuyer's no-negative loan had an L/C of 12.990 percent, the homebuyer's monthly mortgage payments would in fact be based on the 12.990 percent L/C, that will remain there until a downturn in the interest-rate market occurs, and the interest rates start coming back down to a reasonable level.

Nevertheless, the no-negative loan can be a beneficial loan for homebuyers who would like to qualify for a higher property value than they would be able to afford with a fixed-rate loan program, and still not have to be subjected to any deferred interest. Moreover, this loan program allows homebuyers to qualify at the margin and index only, and is also ideal for people who anticipate income increases of 10 percent, or 20 percent or more each year in their work environment. This loan can also be advantageous to homebuyers who only want a short mortgage loan for a period of three to five years, as they know they will be relocating within that time period. The no-negative loan program can also be controlled by homebuyers, as it allows them to limit the amount of their monthly mortgage loan payment increases, providing they know how to work the loan to their advantage. Again, homebuyers need to have a complete understanding of the inner workings of this adjustable loan, and full knowledge of how this loan works before signing any loan documentation.

Next we have the negative or option loan, which also maintains the standard adjustable loan format in that this loan has a "start rate, margin, note rate, index, payment cap and a life cap (L/C)." In order for homebuyers to be able to identify this adjustable loan as a negative or option loan, the loan will indicate that it has a 7.500 percent annual payment-cap increase. However, this adjustable loan may be subject to deferred interest until the loan reaches its current note rate, or wraps any deferred interest back on to the principal loan amount up to a maximum of 1.25% over the initial loan amount that was financed, or when the loan becomes fully indexed.

The negative or option loan is by far the best adjustable loan on the market today, and it is the best mortgage loan available to anyone, as it is the only loan that anyone has the ability to control the way they want, when they want, as many times as they want, as if they were driving a car! However, because this loan program is extremely complex, as well as extremely diversified for the average person to be able to understand the benefits and complexities involved with this particular loan program, I have devoted an extensive section further on in this book for the homebuyer's viewing and understanding concerning this unique, one-of-a-kind adjustable loan program referred to and known as the adjustable negative loan or option loan, or the only loan anyone should ask their lender for providing the lender is offering this loan program.

Let's now view the final adjustable loan, which is known as the graduated-payment mortgage loan (GPM), otherwise known and referred to as the semi-boneless ham loan. Question: is the GPM an adjustable-interest-rate loan? Yes. Question: Is the GPM a fixed-interest-rate loan? Yes. According to the underwriting guidelines of FNMA and FHLMC, the GPM is in fact a fixed-interest-rate loan that also maintains a built-in adjustable-interest-rate variable factor, which is in effect during the first five to seven years of this loan program, depending upon the buyer's decision to select a 5.000 percent or a 7.500 percent payment cap increase for this loan program.

Unlike the standard adjustable loan format, that has a start rate, margin, note rate, index, payment cap, and life cap (L/C), the GPM loan program does not have or maintain a margin, an index, or an L/C, and therefore, the GPM cannot be classified as an official adjustable-interest-rate loan during the initial five to seven years, or until the GPM actually becomes a fixed-interest-rate loan. Readers should now be able to understand why the GPM is known as the semi-boneless ham loan, or they should be totally confused!

Okay, let's simplify the GPM loan program so that we can all have a reasonable understanding of how this loan program works. Like the other two adjustable loans, the GPM has a start rate, note rate, and a 5.000 percent or a 7.500 percent annual payment cap. However, unlike the negative, or option loan, the GPM maintains a built-in guarantee that determines the amount of deferred interest that the GPM can accumulate during the adjustable period of the loan, as established by the underwriting guidelines set forth by both FNMA and FHLMC.

To simplify this even further, even though the GPM is an adjustable negative or deferred-interest loan for the first five to seven years, depending on the loan terms selected by the homebuyers, the GPM principal loan balance cannot increase more than 2 percent or 1.02 percent add on interest on the 5.000 percent payment-cap loan program nor more than 3 percent or 1.03 percent add on interest on the 7.500 percent interest-rate loan program, whereas the negative or option loan could have a principal increase or wrap-around of as much as 1.25% over the original loan amount over a period of five to seven years, depending on how the lender establishes the loan guidelines.

In my professional opinion, the GPM is a superb loan for first-time homebuyers, move-up homebuyers (providing they stay within the conventional conforming loan guidelines), and homebuyers who would like to purchase more property with an adjustable-interest-rate loan but do not have the ability to understand the working advantages of the negative or option loan. Moreover, the GPM loan program will allow the homebuyers to qualify at the start rate depending on the current market interest rate at the time of acceptance. Furthermore, the GPM loan also allows the homebuyers to know five to seven years in advance what their eventual fixed-interest-rate monthly mortgage loan payments will be according to the established note rate, which must be indicated in the homebuyer's loan documentation before he/she agrees to accept the GPM loan program.

To view this from another perspective, when the fixed-interest-rate market on a thirty-year loan is running approximately 8.500 percent to 10.500 percent, then prospective homebuyers would see a very strong adjustable loan market emerge. Likewise, prospective homebuyers should also be able to qualify for not only a higher valued property, but also for a lower interest rate, which in turn would justify the higher value or price of a home that prospective homebuyers could afford. Nevertheless, GPM loan programs will usually disappear from the lending market when the fixed-interest-rate market goes below 7 percent, or at the no-negative adjustable loan note rates, as this seems to be the rule of thumb for qualifying all potential homebuyers for adjustable-interest-rate loans by the lending institutions as required by the OTS and OCC.

The brighter side concerning the adjustable-interest-rate loan is that in the event the fixed-interest-rate market takes a turn for the worse, prospective homebuyers can still buy the home that they desire, and yet they will still have the option to refinance further down the road at a more favorable fixed interest rate if they so desire. In other words, until the adjustable-interest-rate-mortgage-loan payment reaches a level equivalent to the fixed-interest-rate-mortgage-loan market, homebuyers will be enjoying the benefits of the lower monthly mortgage payments of the adjustable loan, as well as, playing on the appreciation value of their home investment. Likewise, homebuyers will be in a much better position (or should be) two to three years down the road to decide whether or not they would like to even consider refinancing their adjustable-interest-rate mortgage loan to a fixed-interest-rate loan.

And finally, there are basically only two things for homeowners to remember when contemplating whether or not to refinance an adjustable home loan: (1) how long do they intend to keep their home? And (2) is their current interest rate at least 1.50 percent to 2 percent above the current fixed-interest-rate market? If the answer to the first question is three to five years or longer, and the answer to the second question is yes, then the homeowners should refinance their home loan for a fixed-interest-rate loan should they so desire. Now, if the answer to the second question is no, then the homeowner should not refinance the home, as he or she will not come out financially, gaining any advantage by refinancing the current home loan even if the lender states that all the points and closing costs will be paid for by the lender. Note—and trust me on this one—even though the lender is willing to pay for the borrower's points and all closing costs, the borrowers will be the ones who will end up paying for all these costs in the long run. Remember, if the deal sounds too good to be true, then it probably is!

Are There Better Loan Programs Available with Lower Start Rates?

Yes and No, depending on whether or not the homebuyers would like an adjustable loan or a fixed-interest-rate loan. Because of the continual changes in the mortgage loan market arena, new fixed-interest-rate mortgage loan programs have surfaced in an attempt to offset the low start rates of the adjustable-interest-rate mortgage loans. Essentially, these new loan programs are fixed-rate programs having three essential factors, that are as follows: (1) these loans are not tied to an index, e.g., the Eleventh District Cost of Funds, the six-month T-bill, the one-year T-bill, the LIBOR, or the National Average Contract Mortgage Rate, (2) there are no margins, and (3) since these loans are classified as fixed-rate loans, they come under the Fannie Mae and Freddie Mac underwriting guidelines.

In today's mortgage-loan market and with all of the new fixed-rate loan programs available, homebuyers may be able to qualify for a fixed-rate loan anywhere from 1 percent to 3 percent below the current thirty-year fixed-rate loan programs. However, homebuyers must also understand that these are short-term loan programs, which means that homebuyers could be subjected to a higher fixed interest rate or even an adjustable interest rate at the end of the term of their mortgage loan, assuming that the homebuyers do not sell or refinance their mortgage loan within the designated term of their loan.

All of the following mortgage loan programs are classified as fixed-interest-rate loans: 20/20, 15/15, 30/10, 30/7, 7/23, 30/5, 5/25, 30/3, 3/27, 30/1, 10/1, 7/1, 5/1, and 3/1. Likewise, most of these loan programs are still available in the mortgage-loan marketplace, but some of them may not be available from time to time, depending on the current interest-rate market. In addition, there are also fixed-interest-rate loan programs which are known as buy-downs; 4-3-2-1, 3-2-1, 2-1-0, 1-0, and step-rate programs (semi-annual or annual), bimonthly loan programs, equity express loans, equity builder loans, line-of-credit loans, equal loans, piggyback loans, interest-only loans, and the above depends on whether or not the homebuyers are looking for a conforming loan, a nonconforming loan, or a jumbo or super jumbo loan program.

All of the aforementioned mortgage loan programs come under the auspices of the fixed-rate loan and guidelines as required by the United States Federal Reserve Board. Furthermore, all of these loan programs are fixed-rate loan programs, and homebuyers should request information concerning the inner-workings of these new loan programs from their mortgage loan consultants, loan officers or lenders in order to determine which mortgage loan program would be the most beneficial for a homebuyer's particular circumstances. Likewise, the majority of these new loan programs are far better than the standard fixed-rate loan, but the homebuyer must be able to fully understand how these mortgage loan programs work in their entirety before accepting or signing any loan documentation.

As a professional mortgage loan consultant, I cannot begin to stress the importance for homebuyers to have the ability to be able to completely understand the inner-workings of the above-mentioned loan programs. Furthermore, and as usual, the lending institutions have managed to screw up the initial meaning of these loan programs to the point that even the majority of the lenders don't understand how these loans function anymore. As an example, let's use the 30/7 and the 7/23 loan programs for an explanation. When these loan programs originally surfaced, the 30/7 simply meant that the loan was fully amortized for thirty years, and was all due and payable in seven years; this is known as a balloon payment. Likewise, the 7/23 loan program was fixed for the first seven years and would convert to either a full twenty-three-year fixed-rate loan or it would convert to an adjustable loan for the remaining twenty-three years.

Now that the lenders have managed to screw up the original meanings of these loan programs, a 30/7 may or may not be subjected to a balloon payment, and may in fact convert to an adjustable-interest-rate loan. Likewise, the 7/23 loan program may or may not become a fully amortized loan after the initial seven-year period, but may in fact become a balloon payment loan program. Based on this information, the reader can now see why it is so important for homebuyers to have a complete understanding of the inner-workings of these loan programs so as to avoid getting involved in a foreclosure action in the future, because they did not completely understand how these loan programs really functioned, as they were only given a basic or surface understanding or explanation of how the loan programs functioned. I am sure that everyone has heard of the term *buyer beware*; in this situation, where a complete understanding of any unusual mortgage loan programs come into contemplation on behalf of the homebuyers, the homebuyers cannot afford to become involved in latent ambiguity in which one party interprets or understands differently from the other party in the explanation process of these loan programs.

What Is a Conversion-Option Loan?

A conversion-option loan is a no-negative adjustable loan, that may be converted to a fixed interest rate loan in months thirteen through sixty, or months twenty-four through sixty, depending on the lender's particular guidelines concerning the loan program. Furthermore, if the lender is offering a twenty-four- through sixty-month conversion option, homebuyers need to understand that the lenders are simply indicating that they intend to make more money for a longer period of time by restricting the homebuyers' ability to convert to a fixed-interest-rate loan than they would, if the homebuyers had the right to convert to a fixed interest rate in months thirteen through sixty.

Nevertheless, these loan programs serve two purposes: (1) they will allow homebuyers to qualify at a lower interest rate and possibly for a greater purchase value than homebuyers would normally be able to qualify for, and (2) in the event a fixed-interest-rate market comes into a range where the homebuyers would feel comfortable, this loan would then allow homebuyers the opportunity to convert to a fully amortized fixed-interest-rate loan.

The primary thing that homebuyers need to remember is that a conversion-option loan is, in essence, nothing more than a refinanced loan with one very important factor, which is, that it gives homebuyers the right to convert to a fixed-interest-rate mortgage loan when they so desire. Should this type of loan appeal to a homebuyer, that homebuyer should be sure to have the lender indicate to them in writing exactly what the conversion-option cost will be to convert the mortgage loan. The conversion-option loan fee should never exceed a total of .250 percent of the remaining loan balance. This would be approximately $250 dollars per $100,000 dollars in direct cost to homebuyers to have their lender convert their loan from an adjustable-interest-rate loan to a fixed-interest-rate mortgage loan. Note: Be sure to have the conversion-option fees stated in the initial loan documents before committing to this loan!

Moreover, any mortgage-interest-rate loan that allows homebuyers to do something to, or requires homebuyers to adjust to sometime in the future, their mortgage-interest-rate loan would technically be classified as a conversion-option loan. These mortgage loans would include the majority of the loans mentioned in the previous section. In other words, something is going to happen or be adjusted in these mortgage loans, with or without the homebuyer's approval that would classify them as being conversion-option mortgage loans.

What Are Negative Loans, and Are They Beneficial?

YES, YES, YES, AND YES!

Contrary to popular belief, the adjustable negative or option loan is by far the most beneficial mortgage loan available in the mortgage loan marketplace today for homebuyers, and has been the loan of preference for years by the investor community. Nevertheless, the reason that this loan has received such a poor reputation is due to the lack of explanation, and understanding of the advantages concerning this loan, as well as, the fact that the term negative immediately implies or suggests that something is wrong with having this type of loan. However, if in fact this is true, then allow me to ask homebuyers a question. Why do approximately 90 percent of the entire loan portfolios of all the major federal savings-and-loan banking institutions encompass the adjustable negative or option loan?

Basically, an adjustable-interest-rate mortgage loan that is subject to negative amortization or deferred interest, is a loan that maintains a monthly payment that is insufficient to allow for any principal or interest reduction to occur. Because of the low starting interest rate or mortgage payment that the homeowners are making each month, and until the adjustments in the starting interest rate cause this loan to reach the established note rate, or the effective interest rate that the homeowners should be making in order to receive a principal-and-interest reduction with each monthly mortgage loan payment, then this adjustable loan may be subjected to accumulating deferred interest that will be added or wrapped around to the current principal if your loan happens to be a negative loan.

Based on the information we have received from the various lending banks in the state of California, approximately 75% of all homebuyers have an adjustable-negative-interest-rate loan, and yet the majority of these homebuyers do not even realize that they have a negative or option loan. Why? Simply because the lenders inform homebuyers that in order to qualify for their new home loan, the homebuyers can only qualify with an adjustable-interest-rate loan, and have not been informed that their adjustable loan is subject to deferred interest. Now, because the homebuyers want their home, they agree to accept the adjustable loan that the lenders are offering, and the homebuyers are notified that they have been approved for their new home loan. The typical response from homebuyers is usually, thank you, along with hundreds of "Hoorays!" However, seldom, if ever, do homebuyers ask any questions of the lender concerning the adjustable-negative-interest-rate loan they just received, which is okay, as 99.99% of the entire lending community could not possibly begin to explain the inner-workings of the adjustable-negative-interest-rate loan program. Likewise, the homebuyers are so happy that they qualified for, and were able to buy their new home; they simply forget to ask the lender any questions concerning the ins and outs of the loan they were just approved for and simply signed the loan documentation without any hesitation.

What was just covered is a typical scenario that takes place every day in the mortgage loan marketplace. The lenders sell homebuyers the loan programs that they make the most money on, and because the lenders maintain very little knowledge as to the inner workings of these adjustable-interest-rate loan programs, and the way these loans functions, the lenders are at a loss when it comes to explaining the multiple benefits these loans may have to offer to homebuyers. To be more explicit and to the point, mortgage loan consultants and loan officers are told to sell these loans to their clients without having any knowledge or understanding of how adjustable-interest-rate loan programs work. Likewise, the banking and lending managers themselves maintain little if any knowledge of how these loans work, but they are instructed to have the mortgage loan consultants and loan officers push these loans on the general home-buying public. Furthermore, and as ironic as it may sound, even the executive echelon in the banking and lending industry maintain very little knowledge or understanding of how these adjustable-interest-rate loan programs function, and other than the fact that they make a lot of money for the banks and lenders, they honestly don't care.

Nevertheless, let's find out whether or not you have an adjustable-interest-rate loan known as a negative or option loan or a no-negative, or payment shock loan. If a homeowner's or homebuyer's adjustable loan program has a payment cap adjustment of 7.50% annually, then they deserve congratulations, because they have the best adjustable-interest-rate-loan in the marketplace, that is known as the negative or option loan. On the other hand, if the adjustable-interest-rate loan program indicates that the loan is subject to a loan-interest-rate cap of 1 percent every six months or 2 percent annually, then the homeowners or homebuyers have what is known as a no-negative, or payment shock loan.

I don't mean to be repetitious, but it is vital that both homeowners and homebuyers understand that the basic difference is that with a negative or option loan, the annual payment cannot exceed a 7.50% increase beyond the previous annual payment, hence the term payment cap. This means the homeowners or homebuyers will have an adjustable loan with a low start rate, which is adjusted to an index plus a margin. The index may be the Eleventh District Cost of Funds, the Six-Month CD, the Six-Month or One-Year Treasury bill, the LIBOR, (known as the London Inter-Bank Offer Rate), or the National Contract Mortgage Rate, etc. However, should the homeowners or homebuyers have the no-negative, or payment shock loan, and a 1 percent six-month or 2 percent annual interest-rate loan cap, then this adjustable loan program will become subject to payment shock, or monthly payment increases of 10 percent every six months or 20 percent once every year until this loan program reaches the note rate. Furthermore, it is also important to know that the no-negative or payment-shock loan must continue to increase in monthly payments as fast as possible, as previously mentioned, as this loan cannot be subjected to any deferred interest.

On the brighter side, the no-negative, or payment shock loan can be beneficial for prospective homebuyers in the initial one or two years of this loan, as they can also qualify for larger loans because of the lower start rates. On the other hand, if homebuyers would like this particular adjustable-interest-rate loan program, then homebuyers should consider the following two important factors: (1) does the no-negative, or payment shock loan have or maintain a conversion option that would allow homebuyers to convert to a fixed-rate loan? And (2) does the lender offer the 2 percent annual adjustment loan as opposed to the 1 percent six-month adjustment loan? As can now be seen, the no-negative, or payment shock loan can be beneficial for homebuyers, but in most cases this loan program can become a major concern, especially, if homebuyers do not understand how this loan program works.

Before concluding this segment on the adjustable-interest-rate loans, let's take a look at the sixteen major advantages the negative or option loan has to offer the home-buying public, followed by a complete breakdown, and an in-depth explanation in relation to each and every major advantage this loan has to offer to all homeowners and homebuyers.

THE LOAN YOU CAN DRIVE LIKE YOUR OWN CAR
AND
DRIVE THE BANKS CRAZY!

1. $5,000 per $100,000 to offset the negative loan deferred interest.

2. Lender must re-amortize your loan, also known as recasting.

3. Lender must reduce your monthly payment.

4. Automatic built-in annual payment-cap protector.

5. Completely assumable loan program.

6. Only 2 percent to 2.50 percent appreciation required to offset any possible accumulated deferred interest.

7. Can purchase more property because of the lower monthly payment.

8. Deferred interest is a pure tax write-off whenever it is paid, keep records.

9. The option to make the lower or higher payment at your discretion when needed.

10. . Lower interest and payment in a declining market by law.

11. You can determine your monthly payment even after fully indexed.

12. Less interest paid on this loan than would be accumulated on a fully amortized thirty-year fixed-rate loan.

13. You maintain the ability to determine the amount of principal reduction you would like to receive at any time throughout the loan term.

14. Homebuyers can determine how long the loan will be negative based on the difference between the start rate and the note rate.

15. Homebuyers can actually determine the amount of profit the bank can make on their loan.

16. Homebuyers can determine the amount of equity buildup they would like to receive at any time throughout the duration of their loan.

Okay, now let's break each one of these advantages down to its simplest form so that everyone will be able to understand and take advantage of the banking lending institutions by turning the tables against them with the option loan and driving them crazy instead of them taking advantage of unsuspecting borrowers. As an example, we will be using a typical California home valued at $650,000, and we will be financing $300,000 for thirty years using the option loan.

1. $5,000 per $100,000 to offset the negative loan.

For talking purposes, let's say you have a $300,000 thirty-year mortgage loan with a starting interest rate of 1.50 percent and a note rate of 6.75 percent. The difference between these two interest rates will determine the amount of deferred interest that this loan will be subjected to. The monthly payment on $300,000 at 1.50 percent would be $1,035.00 (rounded). Reader note: All numbers stated here-in-out will have been rounded either up or down, and the word rounded will not be included. Moving on, the monthly payment on the same $300,000 at the required 6.75 percent would be $1946.00. Simply subtract the difference, and you have $910.00 that is required to be paid on the loan. But because of the option, you can let this amount become deferred interest, which will wrap around to the back of your loan or on to the principal. Over a twelve-month period of time, the total accumulated deferred interest would be $10,925.00 that would be added back onto your loan. Note: the amount of deferred interest at the end of twelve-months will be greater than that which we have indicated due to the fact that we only took the first month of deferred interest of $910.00, and multiplied this figure over a twelve-month period of time. The reason for the additional increase in the overall figure will be due to any and all the deferred interest that accumulates, that will also accumulate additional interest once it has been added back to the principal balance. However, even though the following months deferred interest will be greater, we will not be going through all the required calculations that are needed to get an exact figure, as our explanation should be sufficient enough for the reader to get the general idea of how the defrayment of interest can affect the adjustable negative or option loan.

Now comes the fun part. If you decided that you did not want any amount of the deferred interest to accumulate, and be added back to your loan, simply go to the bank and make a principal-reduction payment in the amount of $10,925.00. By doing so, you close the gap on the amount of deferred interest that the bank can wrap back to your loan. Likewise, if your were to make an additional principal-reduction payment in the amount of $4,075.00 for a total of $15,000, you would completely offset any further deferred interest on this loan, and your loan would no longer be subjected to deferred interest, and would become a fully amortized loan still maintaining the benefits of the option loan. One final note: When making any additional principal-reduction payment, be sure to make a separate check for the payment, and make sure you inform the bank to send you a statement indicating that the principal-reduction payment has been applied by the bank to your loan.

Caution: Lending institutions may attempt to put your principal-reduction payment into an escrow account in an attempt to continue to collect deferred interest. This is illegal! However, should you become subject to this illegal process, feel free to inform the lending bank that you will report them and their activity to the Office of Thrift Supervision (OTS), or the Comptroller of the Currency (OCC), that governs and oversees state-chartered thrift institutions, that includes savings banks, savings-and-loan associations, and the mortgage lending industry in the United States. The OTS maintains four regional offices located in San Francisco, Dallas, Jersey City and Atlanta. Therefore, regardless of what state you live in, should you run into this problem with your bank or lender, simply call the OTS or the OCC, or look them up on the Internet and file your complaint with the appropriate department depending on where you are located in the United States. Note: As far as we know the OCC operates out of Washington, DC.

2. Lender must re-amortize your loan.

This will apply only to the option loan, as no other loan on the market will allow this to take place. Anytime during the term of your loan, you have the right to make principal-reduction payments, whether $100, $500, $1,000, or more, and whether you do this once, twice, or more a year, the lender must re-amortize your loan. However, homebuyers need to read their loan documentation to determine whether or not they can get immediate satisfaction from their lender for their monthly principal reduction payments, or will they have to wait until the anniversary date of their loan? Likewise, homebuyers also need to check if they will be able to get immediate gratification for making a large principal reduction of $5,000.00 or more at anytime throughout the year. In this situation the homebuyers may want to place a call to the OTS or OCC, and ask them this question, as I had to call the OTC at one time because the lending bank tried to deny me of my right to have my principal reduction payment, and monthly loan payment reduced. The reason I called the OTS, was to explain how I tried to make a principal reduction payment of $5,000.00, and was told by the bank lender that I would have to wait until the anniversary date of my loan before I could receive credit for the principal reduction, and the monthly payment reduction. Needless-to-say, the OTS called the lending banks mortgage loan division to verify this information, and the next thing I realized, was that the lending bank immediately applied my $5,000.00 principal reduction payment to my mortgage loan. Likewise, I was getting a call from the lending bank apologizing for their mistake, as the bank was also reducing my monthly mortgage loan payment. Nevertheless, the lending bank found out that there was no such requirement or restrictions in my loan documentation, that stated that the lending bank could make the decision to delay making my principal reduction payment, and reducing my monthly mortgage loan payment. This simply means that the lender has to recalculate my loan, or your loan for that matter, based on the principal-reduction payment(s) you make, but be sure to check your mortgage loan documentation. Now stay with me, as this gets even better!

3. **Lender must reduce your monthly loan payment.**

The reason the lender is required to re-amortize your loan is that once you make any amount of a principal-reduction payment, your loan has to be recalculated because your loan balance has changed. Therefore, your monthly mortgage payment also has to be changed and reduced in order for your loan to continue to be amortized correctly for the remaining duration of your loan. Furthermore, this will occur each and every time you decide to make a principal-reduction payment, providing your mortgage loan documentation states these facts. Okay, if you haven't already figured out what was just explained in number three above, go back and read it again. Did you get it? This simply means that you can actually determine the amount of a monthly payment you would like to make by incorporating a principal-reduction payment. Okay, let's say you don't like the $1035.00 (rounded) monthly payment as indicated in number one. And let's say you want a monthly payment of $700. No problem, simply keep making small or large principal-reduction payments until you get to the monthly payment you desire, and if your mortgage loan documentation allows your lender to deny you a monthly mortgage payment reduction, just remember that you will eventually get the total reductions on the anniversary date of this mortgage loan as required by law.

Moreover, the option loan in number three above also gives you another advantage over any other loan on the market, in that, not only does the lender have to re-amortize your loan and reduce your monthly payment once you make a principal-reduction payment, but you have also increased you equity in your home without having to rely on any so-called appreciation to take place. This in turn not only gives you more equity, but it also increases your borrowing power ability, simply because you made a principal-reduction payment. Now try that with any other loan on the market, and see if you can get all of the above aforementioned benefits. No way, and not even possible! And remember, we are only on number three.

4. **Automatic built-in annual payment-cap protector**

This aspect of the option loan is very important, especially during an inflationary cycle. Because you have an automatic built-in annual payment-cap protector in the form of 7.5 percent regardless of what or where interest rates decide to go, the option loan guarantees your monthly payment from year to year or until your loan becomes fully amortized, that usually occurs at the end of the fifth year, or whenever your loan reaches 1.25 percent of the original loan amount with the accumulated deferred interest. It may be possible for your loan to reach the 1.25 percent maximum allowable wrap-around deferred interest by allowing all of the deferred interest to accumulate, and added back onto the remaining principal balance of this loan, but I have never seen it happen in all the years I have worked as a mortgage loan officer and in all the years that I have had the option loan.

Furthermore, I should also point out that if the option loan should manage to reach the 1.25 percent maximum allowable wrap-around of deferred interest before the loan becomes fully indexed, then the option loan would automatically be re-amortized by the lenders. Therefore, regardless of what may happen with the interest rates in the future, your monthly payments would always be protected by the 7.5 percent annual payment cap, even if the original loan amount reaches the 1.25 percent maximum allowable wrap-around of deferred interest, and assuming the loan remains an option loan after it is re-amortized, so check with your lender. And remember, homebuyers can still become subjected to a monthly mortgage loan payment based on the life cap of the loan in a runaway interest-rate market if they are no longer protected by the annual payment cap. But don't worry, as I will show you how to prevent this scenario from occurring in the following sections.

5. Completely assumable

In the mortgage loan industry there are only two loans (excluding government loan programs) that are completely assumable, and these are the option loan and the no-negative, or payment shock loan. In fact, just for your own edification, there are a ton of acronyms out there in the marketplace, some of which I have indicated in this book, but the fact remains that regardless of the number of acronyms, there are only two adjustable loans in the mortgage marketplace which I have indicated above.

Having a mortgage loan that is completely assumable is a very valuable loan to have in today's home-buying market, because it can make selling your home much easier if the prospective buyers can apply to assume your current loan, and qualify for the balance of the new loan based on the sales price.

6. **Only 2 percent to 2.50 percent appreciation is required to offset any possible accumulated deferred interest that may wrap-around to the principal.**

Let's say that you are happy with your start rate payment and elect not to make the note rate payment on your loan and want to allow the deferred interest to wrap-around to the back of your option loan, but you are concerned about the amount of deferred interest that will be accumulating on your loan. No problem. There is no need to be worried, because it only requires a 2 percent to 2.50 percent market appreciation to offset any possible accumulated deferred interest that may wrap-around and be added to the principal of the option loan.

As our example, let's go back to advantage number one and look at the amount of deferred interest that could accumulate over a twelve-month period of time, and be subject to being added back on to principal of your loan. If you remember, the amount of deferred interest was $10,925.00 for the first twelve months of this loan. Now, do you also remember the sales price of this home? It was $650,000.00. Okay, let's assume an annual home appreciation of only 2 percent, and let's see if this little bit of appreciation will be enough to offset the deferred interest. On the 650,000, 2 percent equals $13,000.00 of appreciation that you would have received for doing nothing at all to your loan, and nothing at all to control the appreciation that occurred, and yet you made $13,000.00 on your home.

Now, if you remember the annual deferred interest was $10,925.00, and you made $13,000 in appreciation, the question is; did you make enough appreciation on your home to offset the amount of accumulated deferred interest? Let's see; $13,000.00 minus $10,925.00 gives us a figure of $2,075.00 of positive cash appreciation even though we allowed the total amount of deferred interest to wrap-around to our option loan. Now remember, this was with only 2 percent of appreciation. What would happen if you received 10 percent, 20 percent or more in appreciation, or just the standard 12.5 percent appreciation we receive every year, most of the time, in California? You would simply make more money in the form of equity in your home, and the deferred interest would basically become negligible.

7. **Can purchase more in property value because of the lower monthly payment.**

This advantage is a little tricky, so I will break it down into simple terms so that everyone will be able to understand how this advantage works, and when to take advantage of it when the home-buying market changes, which it does from year to year in the mortgage loan business. Banks are in the business of lending money, and when they can't make mortgage loans because the general buying public can't afford to buy a home, they have to change the lending rules in order to stay in the lending business.

So this is how advantage number seven works. In the late 1980s and early 1990s, the prices of homes started moving to a point where the average home-buying general public was having a difficult time trying to qualify to purchase a home. Now, as the banks need to continue to make mortgage loans, they had to change the qualifying rules for adjustable-interest-rate loans by allowing homebuyers to qualify at the adjustable loan start rates, or a couple of points above the start rates, instead of requiring homebuyers to qualify at the note rates.

This process accomplished two things for the banks: (1) more people could afford to qualify for a mortgage home loan, and (2) the banks were able to continue to make loans and stay in business.

However, this change also made it possible for potential homebuyers who may have been just marginal, barely able to qualify for a mortgage loan at note rates, to become homebuyers by allowing them to qualify at the start rates. This little adjustment alone, made by the banks, allowed marginal homebuyers to become buyers of homes because of the lower qualifying start rates, that also maintained much lower monthly payments than the traditional fixed-rate loans could offer. Nevertheless, like all good things in life, these loans just didn't seem to stay around very long, and as time went on, and the economy became healthy again, the banks changed the qualifying rules back for the adjustable loans by requiring homebuyers to again qualify at the higher note rates.

Nonetheless, all is still not lost, even though our current mortgage-loan market in our current year is requiring homebuyers to qualify at the adjustable loan note rates, and as the fixed-interest-rate market continues to increase, the option-loan note rates will remain below the fixed interest rates, which has always been the case with adjustable-interest-rate loans. However, according to my sources at the OTS, new loan qualifying guidelines require all lenders to qualify homebuyers at the full index rate, or the option-loan note rate. This means that homebuyers must be able to qualify at the fully indexed interest rate plus amortization. Moreover, according to the source I spoke with at the OTS, it seems that the lenders have submitted a proposal to the OTS asking the OTS to consider allowing the lenders the right to qualify homebuyers, not only at the fully indexed interest rate plus amortization, but also on the balance of the option loan.

Simply put, this means that the lenders would now take the principal loan balance and include the 1.25 percent maximum allowable wrap-around of the deferred interest, and even if the deferred interest doesn't occur, the lenders would still be able to subject the option loan to the possibility of the additional deferred interest and force homebuyers to qualify at an even higher loan amount by adding the 1.25 percent maximum allowable deferred interest wrap-around into the option loan. Personally, I don't believe the OTS will allow this to take place, as the consequences would have a dramatic effect on the home-buying public. For those of you who would like to keep up on this sort of information, or would like to see the OTS guidelines concerning adjustable-interest-rate -loans, you can go to www.ots.gov.com.

The reason for this not occurring is that the current interest-rate market is starting to rise again and fewer and fewer people in the general home-buying marketplace can't afford to purchase a home in the $500,000 or $650,000 range, and afford to make a principal-and-interest payment that was approaching the 7 percent interest-rate market in 2007.

Therefore, something is going to have to give. Either home price's will have to come down as interest rates rise, or the banks are going to have to figure out how to adjust their lending policies in order to accommodate the general home-buying public, and continue to stay in business by making home loans. And even though the current interest for a fixed-rate loan is just about the same as that of an adjustable-interest-rate loan, sooner or later things will have to change in order to allow more people in the general homebuying public to be able to become homebuyers. And finally, one more very important fact remains, which is, that even though fixed-interest-rate loans, and adjustable-interest-rate loans are qualifying at just about the same interest rates, the adjustable-interest-rate option loan still maintains, and will always maintain major advantages over the standard 30-year fixed rate loan that is known as the worst home loan on the market!

8. Deferred interest is a pure tax write-off

This is pretty much self-explanatory, so I will give it a brief overview. Let's say that you are in a position to make the note rate payment on the option loan instead of making the start rate payment. What happens to the deferred interest? Basically, if you make the note rate payment, the amount of deferred interest becomes a pure tax write-off, and your loan will not become subjected to any wrap-around of deferred interest to the principal. In essence, your option loan will function like any standard fixed-rate loan, with the exception that you will receive a considerable amount of tax write-off, depending on the difference between your start rate and note rate, and you will still maintain all of the benefits of the option loan.

Furthermore, it is important to note that with the option loan, you will always have the ability to make the note rate payment at any time throughout the duration of your loan in order to take advantage of the tax write-off. However, it is also important to realize that in the event that you do not allow the deferred interest to wrap-around to the principal, you will not be able to take advantage of the tax write-off. Again, this can only be taken advantage of if you make the note rate payment before the bank can add the deferred interest back to the principal loan amount.

The biggest advantage of number eight will apply to those who find themselves in a high income tax bracket. This is when advantage number eight becomes a superior advantage. Not only will you receive a pure tax write-off when making the note rate payment, but should you also elect to make any kind of principal-reduction payments as well, then you will be controlling this adjustable loan to your advantage, as you will be accomplishing three major points: (1) You get the pure tax write-off of the deferred interest, (2) You will be reducing your principal along with having your loan re-amortized, and your monthly payment reduced, and (3) You will be taking advantage of any appreciation that may take place while you own your home. In other words, you will be taking advantage of the banks, and driving them crazy by making them work your loan over and over again while you sit back and relax and enjoy the benefits of advantage number eight. Furthermore, you will be kicking the heck out of your loan from the bottom up and from the top down, as well as sideways. Try this with any other mortgage loan in the marketplace!

9. **The option to make a lower or higher payment at your discretion**

The primary major advantage of the option loan that no other loans in the marketplace can offer to the homebuyers is the right to make either the note rate payment or the start rate payment anytime throughout the duration that the option loan is subject to deferred interest. This little aspect concerning the option loan makes this the best mortgage loan available in the home loan market for every homebuyer, because it allows homebuyers to make their own determination as to whether or not they want to make the higher note rate payment, or the lower start rate payment whenever they have the desire or need to switch from one mortgage payment to another. Before

I show you how this process can work to your advantage, I would also like to point out that the option loan is extremely advantageous to those people who occasionally make large amounts of money at different times throughout the year, and for those who work on commissions as opposed to those who work as employees.

Okay, here we go. Let's say that you bought your home and the bank gave you the option loan, but did not tell you anything about all of the advantages the loan has to offer, which usually happens, as the majority of the banking and mortgage lending industry doesn't have the slightest idea of how this loan works, but they do know that they can qualify more homebuyers with this loan, and so they continue to sell it to the unsuspecting public, who also has no idea of what you can do with the option loan, but I will change all of that for everyone right now.

As I have previously mentioned, if you are currently in a high-income bracket and need a write-off, simply make the note rate payment, and write off the deferred interest. On the other hand, let's say you can afford to make the start rate payment when you begin repaying the loan, but you realize that you will be getting an increase in your income in the future, and you will then be able to make the note rate payment or you can decide to make principal-reduction payments. The way you decide to go is strictly your decision, and your right as long as you have the option loan.

Furthermore, let's say that your family has two incomes and everything is going great, and you are currently making the note rate payment every month on your mortgage loan, and then *boom!* Something happens to one of the income earners that puts one of them out of work or in the hospital, and you can no longer continue to make the note rate payment on your mortgage loan. Can you then start making the lower start rate payment? You bet your life you can, and you can do so for as long as you like without having to worry about receiving foreclosure notices from your lender. Now, let's say the other household income earner gets back on his/her feet five or six months down the line, and begins doing business and making money as usual. Can you then return to making the note rate payments on your mortgage loan? Again, you can bet your life on it, and you can do this for as long as you like. This is the beauty of the option loan. And remember, as long as you have the option loan as your mortgage loan, you can switch back and forth as many times as you want without becoming subjected to any legal repercussions whatsoever. Now, try that with any other loan in the marketplace and see what happens to your home!

10. **Lower interest and payment in a declining market**

This is another great feature of the option loan, and it is one that you don't have to concern yourself with, as your interest and monthly mortgage payments will automatically be adjusted downward in a declining interest-rate market. Basically, when the interest-rate market declines, the option loan interest rates decline thereby closing the gap between the note rate and the start rate. This means that the banks must recalculate your mortgage loan interest rate, which will affect the deferred interest you would have been subjected to, and because of the declining interest-rate market, you will see a further reduction in your monthly mortgage loan payment.

This entire process will be taken care of automatically by the lender holding or servicing your mortgage loan and you will simply receive monthly notices indicating that your monthly mortgage payment has been lowered, and that you are to make the new lower payment on your mortgage loan. This process can go on for a period of months, and each month you would receive a notice from your lender indicating the new lowered monthly mortgage loan payment. Note: this process will affect both the note rate and the start rate payments regardless of which payments you are making on your mortgage loan.

Likewise, in an increasing interest-rate mortgage market, you don't have to be concerned, as the option loan maintains a built-in payment cap that will not allow your mortgage loan payments to increase any more than 7.5 percent per annum.

Furthermore, homebuyers can also take additional advantage of this process with the option loan. As an example, I will use an actual option loan that I had a few years ago. At that time my wife and I were making our mortgage loan payments based on the start rate when the interest-rate market started to decline. We began getting statements from our lender every month, for a period of seven months, informing us that we were to make the new lower mortgage loan payments as the interest market continued to decline. Over the seven-month period, our payments went down over $600 per month, and we were ecstatic.

However, instead of us starting to make the newer and lower monthly note rate payment with these newfound monies, we decided to start making monthly principal-reduction payments with the extra $600, and began to knocking down our principal on our option loan. As we continued to knock down the principal loan amount because of the reduction in the interest-rate market, the interest-rate market finally reached its bottom after seven months and managed to stay at a low interest rate for an additional fifteen months before the interest rates started to rise again.

Needless to say, we knocked down our principal loan amount by a whopping $12,600.00 with this free money because of the declines in the interest-rate market. Likewise, even though the interest-rate market started to climb again, my wife and I found out that our monthly mortgage payments were not increasing as we thought they would. We had discovered, strictly by accident, that by making the principal-reduction payments with these new found monies over twenty-one months, we had managed to completely offset the deferred interest that our option loan had previously been subjected to. In other words, we were no longer subjected to any deferred interest, and yet we still maintained all of the advantages of the option loan.

The reason I related the above information to you is not only to show you how to use this advantage to your benefit, but also to show you how you can use this information against the lenders, thereby offsetting or even eliminating the possibility of being subjected to any deferred interest concerning the option loan. Furthermore, the decision to take advantage of a situation like this will be up to you if the interest-rate loan market takes a downward turn like it has started again since 2007 through 2015. Likewise, we requested another negative adjustable loan for our new home, and again we have been using the major advantages this loan offers to where our current monthly mortgage payment is now 35.00. Furthermore, we are now at the point in December of 2014 where we intend to make another principal reduction payment that should, according to my calculations, reverse the principal and interest that the bank has been making, to where we will now be receiving more principal on our mortgage payments, and the bank will be making less on the interest payments starting on the anniversary of our option loan in 2015. If this process works the way I have figured, it will be great to know that one can turn the tables on the lending banks, and browbeat them out of their loan interest instead of the other way around. Not bad!

11. You can determine your monthly mortgage payment even after fully indexed

So that everyone will understand what I am talking about concerning the term *fully indexed,* I will take a few lines to explain what it means. Simply put, it means that your option loan is no longer subject to any deferred interest and your loan is fully amortized for its remaining duration. Likewise, throughout the remaining duration of your option loan, anytime you would like to know what your current effective interest rate is, just simply take the number from the index you agreed to, and add it to the margin and you will come up with the current interest rate governing your mortgage loan. Again, this process of becoming fully indexed usually takes approximately five years, depending on which index you accepted at the time of signing for your new home loan. Furthermore, depending how the lender calculates your monthly mortgage loan payments, and assuming that your loan does not wrap-around the maximum deferred interest amount allowable by law of 1.25 percent where your loan automatically becomes fully indexed, or you could end up going as much as five years before your loan becomes fully indexed, depending on the difference between your start rate and note rate, and assuming that you decide not to work your option loan as you are being instructed. Moreover, all banks will automatically recast the option loan at five years with the exception of World Savings and Loan, located in California, which recasts at ten years. Note: World Savings and Loan that was located in California, was bought out by Wachovia Bank N. A., Headquartered in Charlotte, North Carolina. Having spoken with personnel at Wachovia Headquarters, I was pleased to learn that Wachovia will continue to offer the option loan, and service the loans that were acquired by World Savings and Loan under the Wachovia name. Note: Wachovia Bank N. A. is no longer in business, and was taken over by Wells Fargo Home Mortgage Loan Division. However, the Wells Fargo Home Mortgage Loan Division is subjected to honoring the original mortgage loan contracts that were originally established by World Savings and Loan, and any loans that were issued by Wachovia Bank N. A. This means, that the Wells Fargo Home Mortgage Loan Division cannot in anyway implement their rules, or guidelines into any of the home loan mortgage contracts that they inherited, by taking over these previously established mortgage loans from World Savings and Loan or Wachovia Bank N. A.

This simply means that once your option loan becomes fully indexed, you will still maintain the right to make principal-reduction payments anytime you decide throughout the duration of the loan, which in turn, will continue to reduce your monthly mortgage payments until you are satisfied with your payment. Again, try this with any other loan in the marketplace and see what your lender will think about it!

12. **Less interest paid on this loan than would be accumulated on a fully amortized thirty year fixed rate loan.**

Normally, fixed-interest-rate loans will usually have higher interest rates than most interest start rates on the option loan, and even the interest rates on the note rates will usually be lower, as the interest-rate market doesn't sit still for any length of time before it starts moving up or down again. Therefore, as a rule, homebuyers who elect to have the option loan, as opposed to a fixed-interest-rate loan will always pay less interest over the long term of their mortgage loan. The reason that this happens, is that whether interest rates are high or low, the option loan is designed to allow less interest to be paid on the loan in the beginning years of the loan, and to remain that way until the loan becomes fully indexed. However, by the time the option loan becomes fully indexed, fixed-interest-rate loans will continue to go higher or lower by 2 percent to 3 percent as the option loan tends to remain the same. Likewise, because the mortgage loan interest-rate market is constantly changing, and the option loan is protected by the annual 7.5 percent payment cap, homebuyers will end up paying less overall interest throughout the duration of the option loan whether or not homebuyers elect to work their option loan.

Another important aspect of the option loan that comes into play, especially, in the beginning years of the loan, is the amount of mortgage interest being paid will be considerably less as compared to that of a fixed-interest-rate loan. Furthermore, one must remember that the average length of time that people live in their homes in today's marketplace is between five and seven years. Keeping this in mind, one can understand why the option loan is a superior mortgage loan as opposed to any fixed-interest-rate loan in the marketplace. Moreover, once you have viewed the fixed-interest-rate loan breakdown, that I have included for your information, you will be astonished to realize just how much equity you will have accumulated over a five-year period of time, not to mention the accumulated equity buildup you will have received over a ten-, fifteen-, or twenty-year period of time with a fixed-rate loan.

Another major downfall of having a fixed-interest-rate loan is that not only do you not receive any substantial equity buildup in the first twenty years of your fixed-rate loan, but there is also no way to work the fixed-rate loan to your advantage. Sure, you can make principal-reduction payments anytime you decide throughout the duration of the loan, but what will it get you? Your monthly mortgage payment will not become lower, and sure, you will reduce the total time for payoff by about two to four years, assuming that you continue to make monthly principal-reduction payments. However, if the average homebuyer lives in a home for only five to seven years, what good would it do to reduce your principal amount? Nevertheless, the point being made is that if you haven't already figured out how great the option loan really is, then this is just another advantage to add to the list.

13. **You maintain the ability to determine the amount of principal reduction you would like to receive at any time**

Even though I have mentioned this advantage in several of the aforementioned advantages, this still remains a major advantage. Therefore, I will give it a brief overview to make sure everyone understands the importance of having access to this advantage.

Let's say your option loan has now become fully indexed and you are five or more years into the mortgage loan. Can you still continue or begin to make principal-reduction payments with this loan? Yes! Even though your option loan has become fully indexed, you still have an option loan, which entitles you to continue to take advantage of this advantage anytime throughout the duration of the loan. Remember, anytime you decide to make a principal-reduction payment, your lender has to recast your loan and reduce your monthly mortgage payment, providing your loan documentation indicates this process can take place. However, even though you can make a principal reduction at anytime, you may or may not be allowed, or entitled to the monthly mortgage payment reduction, so be sure to check your loan documentation. If this happens to be your situation, you can only do one or two things: 1) You can wait until the anniversary date of your loan when everything will be reduced or 2) You can place a call to the OTS or OCC, and ask them to check with your banks mortgage loan division to see if your mortgage loan contract indicates or states that these reductions can or cannot take place when making principal reductions.

14. **Homebuyers can determine how long the loan will be negative based on the difference between the start rate and the note rate.**

The greater the difference is between the start rate and the note rate, the longer the option loan will remain subject to deferred interest. However, homebuyers have the ability to limit the length of time that an option loan will be subject to deferred interest by simply electing to close the gap between the start rate and the note rate.

This is how it works. Let's take a look back at advantage number one and note the start rate and the note rate percentages that were indicated. If you remember, we had a start rate of 1.50 percent and a note rate of 6.75 percent that we used to calculate our monthly mortgage loan payment. Now, what would happen if you were able to make a start rate payment of say 2.50 percent or 3.75 percent or 4.75 percent or even greater? Did you notice what happened between the difference of the start rate and the note rate? You closed the interest-rate gap, thereby causing the lender to calculate a lesser period of time that would be required to completely offset any negativity of the option loan. Likewise, you also limited the lender to the amount of deferred interest that lender is entitled to wrap-around to the principal loan balance of your mortgage loan.

To make sure that everyone is be able to understand just follow along. We are going to use the start rate of 3.75 percent as an example, and we will now calculate the new start rate payment using the start rate vs. note rate payment of 6.75 percent as indicated to see just exactly what I am talking about concerning the option loan. Using the new start rate of 3.75, amortized over thirty years based on financing $300,000, we get a monthly mortgage start rate payment of $1,389.00 vs. the note rate payment of $1946.00. Now let's subtract the difference of the start rate payment of $1,389.00 from the note rate payment of $1946.00, and we get a monthly figure of $556.00, which is subject to becoming deferred interest. Likewise, your mortgage loan could only be subjected to wrapping around approximately $6,677.00 to the principal balance of your mortgage loan during the first year of the start rate interest.

Now, if you remember from advantage number one, using the start rate payment at 1.50 percent interest vs. the note rate payment at 6.75 percent interest, you can now see a substantial difference in the amount of deferred interest the lender could have collected in the first year of the option loan had you chosen the 1.50 percent start rate vs. the 3.75 percent start rate. As you can see, the maximum annual wrap-around of deferred interest went from $10,925.00 at 1.50 percent down to $6,677.00 for the deferred interest subject to a wrap-around at 3.75 percent, or a savings to you of $4,248.00 in the first year of your start rate payment simply because you elected the higher start rate payment vs. the note rate payment. Furthermore, by choosing the higher start rate payment, you also limited the amount of time the option loan can be subjected to deferred interest.

Note: This is vitally important to learn, know, and remember. Choosing a higher start rate payment with an option loan must take place in the beginning of the loan process, as you will not be able to make any changes once your loan is approved.

15. Clients can actually determine the amount of profit the bank can make on their loan.

There are three ways homebuyers can determine or limit the amount of profit a bank is able to make on an option loan. However, before I cover this advantage, it's important for the reader to realize that the option loan is an extremely profitable loan for the banks and other portfolio lenders. Note: A portfolio lender is one that not only makes the loan to homebuyers, but also services or collects the monthly mortgage loan payments until the option loan becomes fully indexed. Again, this usually takes five or more years, as was previously discussed, at which time the portfolio lenders sell your loan in the secondary mortgage-loan market, as the option loan no longer maintains its profitability because the banks take out all of the major profitability the option loan has to offer before it becomes re-amortized for the remaining duration of the loan.

The primary reason for this profitability is that the lenders do not or will not tell homebuyers anything about the option loan for a couple of reasons, that are as follows: (1) the lenders know very little about the option loan (this is usually the case), or (2) the lenders realize how profitable the option loan is before it becomes fully indexed. Therefore, if the lenders do know anything about how one could take advantage of this loan, other than the fact that it is an easy loan to qualify for and usually allows for a lower credit score, they are definitely not going to reveal this information to homebuyers, as this information would affect their profitability.

Okay, let's look at the three ways homebuyers can limit the profitability of the option loan. The first way, which I already discussed in detail in advantage number fourteen, is to close the gap between the start rate and the note rate. The second way is to buy down the margin. The opportunity to buy down the margin is seldom if ever talked about by portfolio lenders, as this is the primary source of their profitability. To put this information another way, simply means that as long as the option loan remains active and does not become fully indexed and amortized; the portfolio lender makes the point spread on the margin each and every month. Stay with me on this, as this is how it works. The margin is the fixed aspect of the option loan, and the index is the variable, or fluctuating, aspect of the adjustable-interest-rate loan. Now, the portfolio lenders maintain absolutely no control over any of the indexes that they may be offering to homebuyers and therefore, there are no monies available to the lenders via the indexes. However, the lenders do make a tremendous amount of monies based on the option loan each and every month they collect the monthly mortgage loan payments.

In other words, let's say that your option loan maintains a margin of 2.95, 3.25, 3.75, or a higher percentage. These figures represent the fixed aspect of the option loan, as well as the monthly profit to the portfolio lenders, that gets added to the index, that in turn establishes the effective interest rate you should be paying on the option loan in order to keep the loan from accruing deferred interest, that is known as the note rate. The entire adjustable loan program, and all of the terms are explained in another section of this book. Therefore, suffice it to say, that as long as the option loan remains active and does not become fully amortized, then the portfolio lenders will continue to make their extra monies on your loan each and every month based on the amount of the margin, but the lenders are not going to tell you or let you know that you have the right to buy the down the margin. Furthermore, before you sign any loan documents, be sure to buy down the margin if you so desire because once the loan documents are signed, you can no longer buy down the margin. Now, you have already probably figured out that the lower the margin the less profit the portfolio lenders will be able to make. And, like everything else in life goes, if you intend to limit the profit to the portfolio lenders, there will definitely be a high price to pay in order to get a lower margin.

Buying down a margin can be a very expensive proposition, simply because you are cutting and dealing with lenders' profits. However, after extensive research, I found the buy-down rates to cost one point of your loan amount to buy down a half point of the margin, and a cost of two points to buy the margin down a full point. However, this is just a rule of thumb, as some lenders were a little higher and some were just a little lower in their buy-down rates, and some lenders didn't even want to discuss the subject. Nevertheless, it's important to understand and remember that one point in the loan industry is equivalent to 1 percent, two points is equivalent to 2 percent, and so forth. Therefore, let's say we had a margin of 3.50 percent and we wanted to buy the rate down a half point. Using our loan amount of $300,000 as indicated in advantage number one, it would cost $3,000 to lower the margin to 3.00 percent at a one-point cost. Likewise, if you decided to lower the margin down another half point to get a margin of 2.50, it would cost you $6,000 to reduce the points from 3.50 percent to 2.50 percent

As you can see, it can become quite costly to buy down the margin on an option loan, but remember, you are taking away the profit from the lenders, and because they are in the business of making money, they will do whatever they can to discourage you from attempting to buy down the margin. Nevertheless, according to the persons I spoke with at OTS, there are no rules or regulations to stop homebuyers from negotiating buy-down rates on the margin. Therefore, and again according to the OTS, should you, the homebuyers, decide to negotiate a margin buy-down with your lender, and the lender refuses to listen or agree to allow you to buy down the margin, then find another lender that will. Furthermore, if you want to make life miserable for the lender who refused to discuss a margin buy-down, you could simply report them to the OTS or the OCC, and depending on which one you call either one will conduct an investigation into the lending practices of the lender in question. Furthermore, the majority of lenders will avoid the subject with you if they can, and elude the fact that you have the right to buy down the margin, and now you know why.

The third way homebuyers can determine or limit the amount of profit the banks are able to make on an option loan has to do with the life cap. Basically, the life cap is the ceiling, or the maximum amount of interest that an adjustable loan can become subjected to over any given period of time. Even in a runaway inflationary interest-rate market the adjustable loans cannot exceed their life caps. Incidentally, life caps are relatively new to the adjustable loan market, as in the 1980s the adjustable loans, graduated-payment loans, and a myriad of other non-fixed-rate loans did not maintain any sort of life caps, and in 1982, especially in California, when the interest-rate market went over 23 percent, the foreclosure rate skyrocketed, and the number of bankruptcies went through the roof, all because none of these adjustable or graduated payment loans maintained any form or guideline concerning a life cap. It was during this period of time that homebuyers could get into homes easily by qualifying at the lower start rates or at the lower graduated-payment loan start rates. These were the loans that were being pushed by the lenders onto the unsuspecting homebuyers at that time, and only for the unsuspecting homebuyers to find out that one month their mortgage loan might be $800, the next $1,200, the next $1,800, and so on until the people simply lost their homes or walked away from them and left the state.

At that time the Federal Home Loan Bank Board was the governing body over the federally chartered and state-chartered savings-and-loans, banks, and other lenders. However, after the fallout of 1982, the Federal Home Loan Bank Board had to act fast to establish some new lending guidelines to keep this sort of disaster from ever happening again, hence the formal inauguration of the life interest-rate cap, or as we call it in the lending industry, the life cap. Note: The Federal Home Loan Bank Board was disbanded a few years ago after this debacle occurred, and on August 9, 1989, the OTS replaced the Federal Home Loan Bank Board as the primary regulator of all federally chartered and state-chartered savings and loans, banks, and other lenders.

The life cap is not a big advantage factor, as all non-fixed-rate loans maintain some form of a life cap. However, getting the lowest life cap can become an important factor, especially, in an inflationary interest-rate-driven market. Question: Can homebuyers buy down a life cap? Sure they can; but again, only at the beginning of the loan process and before any loan documentation has been signed. And remember, you are playing around with a lender's ability to make money, so this buy-down can also become very expensive.

So, how do lenders calculate life caps for loans? That's a great question that has no direct answer. Lenders must follow the lending guidelines established by the OTS, and are therefore limited to the amount of excess interest they can add to the life caps. However, the norm is usually four to six points higher than the start rate or the note rate. Even though this doesn't seem like much, remember that the lenders are in business to make money, which will make the following explanation very important for homebuyers to understand.

As an example, let's say the lenders are allowed to charge five points more than the start rate or the note rate. Understand that there are currently no guidelines established by the OTS that regulate lenders as to whether or not they can add five points to the start rate or the note rate to establish a life cap but who knows, maybe this book will inspire the OTS to change the guidelines for the benefit of homebuyers in the near future. Now, in order for the homebuyer to understand this equation, let's say the lenders decide to add the five points to the note rate, and using our example in advantage number one, the lenders add the five points to 6.75 percent to get a life cap of 11.75 percent, or the maximum amount of interest that a homebuyer could be subjected to paying on their mortgage loan. Next we are going to use the same figures, except this time, we are going to add the five points to the start rate of 1.50 percent, which now gives us 6.50 percent as a life cap. Which life cap would you, as a homebuyer, like to pay as a maximum interest rate on your loan?

Why would the lenders be more inclined to add the five points to the note rate in the above example as opposed to adding the five points to the start rate? Did you figure it out? It's simple. The current note rate is already at 6.75 percent, so why would the lenders offer a lesser life cap? On the other hand, let's say the start rate was 2.75 percent, and the lender added the five points. We would then have an effective life cap of 7.75 percent, which would be a good life cap figure. Normally, the higher the start rates are, the better the odds are that the lenders will add their point spread to the start rate to establish the life cap of a mortgage loan. On the other hand, in the above example, the lenders could not afford to offer a life cap that would be lower than the note rate, as they would not be in a position to make any money in the event the interest-rate market continued to move upward; hence the 11.75 percent life cap.

As far as attempting to buy down a margin is concerned, this is a very touchy subject with the lenders, but homebuyers have the right to negotiate a buy-down on the life cap the same as they do with the margin. Moreover, if I had my way, lenders would not be allowed to charge more than three or four points maximum in order to establish a life cap based on the start rate on an adjustable-interest-rate loan, and no more than three points could be added to the note rate on an adjustable loan, as this is simply more profit for the banks and lenders than is necessary.

16. **Clients can determine the amount of equity buildup they would like to receive at any time throughout the duration of their loan**

I have already covered this material quite extensively in some of the above aforementioned advantages, so I will give this advantage a brief overview. The option loan gives homebuyers the right to make principal-reduction payments throughout its entire duration of amortization. Therefore, anytime anyone would like to increase his or her equity buildup with the option loan, he/she can simply make principal-reduction payments and take advantage of building up home equity. Remember, homebuyers can control this loan, so rather than waiting around to see what appreciation and additional equity may have occurred in the real-estate market, during any given year, making additional principal-reduction payments (when you can afford to) will only increase your home equity position.

Now you can see why the option loan not only gives homebuyers sixteen major advantages, but it also gives them the ability to control their mortgage loan, and to manipulate their loan as they desire anytime they want throughout the full term of amortization. Currently, there are no other mortgage loans in the marketplace that would remotely allow one to manipulate like one can with the option loan. Likewise, the majority of lenders throughout the United States offer this loan, and they will usually offer it to marginal homebuyers. However, anyone can ask a lender for an option loan, and should your lender not offer such a loan, simply go to the ones who do and submit your application to those banks or mortgage lenders. Remember, the option loan was taken off the mortgage market after the financial debacle and is currently not available. However, as more and more potential homebuyers start requesting that they have access to the adjustable negative or option loan, the more likely lenders are to start offering this loan again to the home buying public.

Okay, out of all the sixteen major advantages, which one is the most important? Sorry, but all sixteen major advantages are important. However, if you wanted to work just a few aspects of the option loan, then I would suggest using advantages eleven, thirteen, and sixteen, because even though they are used for different reasons, all three maintain the same common denominator, which is the principal-reduction-payment process.

Let's say homebuyers are not in a position to buy down the margin, as they do not want to close the gap between the start rate and note rate at such an expense, and they are not interested in paying the deferred interest the option loan may become subjected to, because of the difference between the start rate and note rate, and yet they want to take advantage of this loan. Principal-reduction payments are the only way to go, even if it takes a little longer, and here's why. Homebuyers can accomplish and obtain all of the above mentioned results simply by making direct principal-reduction payments anytime they can afford to, and in any amount of money they can afford to spare. By doing so, homebuyers will not only be reducing their home principal balance, but they will also be cutting the profits of the lenders in all the above categories.

Here's what will happen when homebuyers make direct principal-reduction payments: (1) It causes the lenders to reduce the mortgage loan principal, which in turn reduces the amount of overall interest the lenders will be able to charge, (2) even though the gap between the start rate and note rate will remain the same, the amount of deferred interest will become less and less because of the reduction of the principal loan balance, (3) the lenders will be forced to reduce the monthly mortgage loan payments, as the gap between the start rate and note rate will be declining because of the principal reduction and the constant re-amortization of the option loan, (4) because of the principal-reduction payments being made, homebuyers will end up paying far less overall interest than they would if they had a fixed-interest-rate loan, (5) the time period for the option loan to remain negative or subject to deferred interest will be dramatically shortened, (6) homebuyers will determine the amount of profit the lenders can make on the option loan, (7) homebuyers will continue to reap all of the additional advantages indicated, without having to do anything to gain the advantages, and finally, (8) homebuyers will have the ability to manipulate the option loan to their satisfaction at any time, and in any way that they choose, because they will have a mortgage loan that will allow them to

DRIVE A LOAN LIKE THEIR OWN CAR

AND

DRIVE THE BANKS CRAZY!

What Is the Worst Home Loan on the Market?

The answer to this question will depend on how long homebuyers plan to live in their home. In other words, according to the National Association of Realtors (NAR) and the California Association of Realtors (CAR), average homeowners will buy and sell their home within five to seven years. Therefore, if this is an accurate statistic, then the worst home loan on the market would be the thirty-year fixed-rate loan!

Now, before homebuyers, homeowners, or anyone else who has a fixed-interest-rate loan goes into a tizzy, allow me to explain the facts concerning the thirty-year fixed-rate loan from an analytical point of view based on a logical analysis. Assuming that the statistics indicated by NAR and CAR are accurate concerning the resale of property, there would be absolutely no advantage for anyone to have a thirty-year fixed-rate loan. Why? Because the equity buildup in the thirty-year fixed-rate loan would be zip—nada--nothing—to homebuyers during the average ownership period of five to seven years; this would actually extend for a period of fifteen years.

Let's take an analytical look at the thirty-year fixed-rate loan and use a logical analysis as it relates to a home purchase having a sale price of $200,000 using a down payment of 10 percent, and financing $180,000 amortized over a thirty-year period of time at an 8.500 percent fixed interest rate. However, the first thing that homebuyers would have to know would be, how to separate interest from the principal in the monthly mortgage payments in order to determine the actual principal reduction that would occur, each and every year that they plan to live in their home. The calculation process is relatively simple, but you need to remember you are only calculating the principal-and-interest payment in this situation. Therefore, in the above scenario we have a monthly mortgage principal-and-interest payment of $1,384.00. Now we take the amount financed, $180,000.00, and multiply this number by the interest rate of 8.50 percent to get an annual figure of $15,300.00, that we again divide by twelve (for twelve months) to get an interest-only figure of $1,275.00. Now we simply subtract the interest-only figure from the principal-and-interest figure of $1,384.00, and we get a principal-reduction figure of $109.00, and we paid $1,275.00 in interest, based on the first month's mortgage payment.

Okay, let's now view the thirty-year fixed-rate loan in increments of five years over a period of fifteen years, based upon the aforementioned loan amount. To keep this simple and to the point, homebuyers will have paid approximately $83, 042.00 in monthly mortgage loan payments, received approximately $8,117.00 in direct principal reduction, and paid approximately $74,925.00 in interest payments alone. In other words, homebuyers will have received 1.05 percent in actual principal reduction applied to their home mortgage loan over a period of five years, which equates to an equity buildup of just over of 1 percent.

In the next five-year period, which would equate to a total of ten years, homebuyers will have paid monthly mortgage loan payments of approximately $166,085.00, received approximately $20,515.00 in direct principal reduction, and they paid approximately $145,570.00 in interest payments. Moreover, homebuyers will have received an actual principal reduction, or an equity buildup of approximately 1.13 percent in their mortgage loan over a period of ten years.

Now, if the aforementioned is not convincing enough in and of itself, let's view our final analysis over the next five-year period, assuming homebuyers intend to live in their home for fifteen years, and chose to finance their home with a thirty-year fixed-rate loan. From a logical and analytical point of view, homebuyers will have made monthly mortgage loan payments of approximately $249,127.00, receiving approximately $39,449.00 in principal reduction, and they will have paid approximately $209,678.00 to the lender just in the form of interest-only payments. Furthermore, a homebuyers' actual total principal reduction would equate to approximately 1.28 percent in equity build up per year over a period of fifteen years, and assuming they opted for and selected a thirty-year fixed-rate loan.

Now remember, this loan still has another fifteen years of payments to be made, which will bring the total interest payments that one will end up paying to the banks to approximately $318,254.40 for an $180,000 loan based on a purchase price of only $200,000. And, to make matters even worse, the total repayment figure would be approximately $498,254.00 and the total amount of interest paid, as a percentage of the principal, would be approximately 176.808

percent. Now, I don't know about you as a homebuyer, but I think that paying close to 200 percent in interest-only payments to a bank for a home loan is just a little too much for my taste. Likewise, the higher the interest rate the greater the percentage to the banks with the thirty year fixed-rate loan.

Based upon the analysis above, why would anyone opt for, select, or desire to choose a thirty-year fixed-rate loan? Before I give you the answer to this question, let's look at the advantages and disadvantages of the thirty-year fixed-rate loan.

ADVANTAGES

1) Security of knowing monthly payment will not change.

2) Ability to make additional principal-reduction payments, but the monthly mortgage loan payment remains the same.

3) Ability to plan life around ball-and-chain payments.

4) Ability to reduce payoff factor to twenty-one or twenty-three years based on number two above.

5) Ability to write off the massive interest that is being charged by the lenders and paid by the homeowners.

DISADVANTAGES

1) No ability to offset the loan.

2) No ability to have monthly payments reduced.

3) Loan is not assumable.

4) No reasonable equity buildup in loan for a period of fifteen plus years.

5) Must rely on appreciation in order to increase equity.

6) Limited to the dollar amount of property that can be purchased.

7) No ability to determine monthly payments.

8) Must make payments even in a reverse and declining property market.

9) More interest being paid on this loan versus other loan programs.

10) No ability to determine the amount of profit paid to the lenders.

As the reader can see, the advantages of the thirty-year fixed-rate loan have been outweighed by a two-to-one ratio by the disadvantages.

Therefore, I can now address the answer to the original question, which was, why would anyone opt for, select, or desire to choose a thirty-year fixed-rate loan?

Even though the answer is relatively simple, it has become extremely complicated because of a myriad of unknown circumstances that have been caused by a lack of understanding, knowledge, education, and propaganda indoctrination, which has been instituted by the banking institutions upon the public since the 1940s. In other words, the banking institutions promoted and continue to promote the security aspect of having a thirty-year fixed-rate loan, and a fixed payment to the unsuspecting homebuyers without offering any explanation to homebuyers concerning the incredible profitability the banking institutions are making, receiving, and realizing by offering the thirty-year fixed-rate loan, all to the detriment of the home-buying public. Why? Simple!

GREED!

Nevertheless, the home-buying public should know, understand, and realize that there is a multitude of better thirty-year amortization fixed-rate loan programs available to all potential homebuyers (please refer to the section entitled "Are There Better Loan Programs Available with Lower Start Rates?), that can be customized to the benefit of homebuyers, that can, and at the same time, limit the amount of profit that the banking institutions will be able to receive over any given term, or length of time concerning any home loan mortgage financing.

Now, should anyone who has read this section still have any questions as to what is the worst home loan on the market, then I suggest rereading the entire section and doing the calculations yourself using your own thirty-year fixed-rate loan amount as your example.

In my professional opinion, if the majority of the general home buying public knew about the major advantages of the option loan and understood how to work the loan to their advantage, the majority of the homeowners throughout the United States of America would now own their own homes outright, and not have to be concerned with what is going on in the housing marketplace.

Allow me to give the reader a real example of buying a home using advantage three of the option loan, that also affects advantages thirteen, fifteen and sixteen, and making the option loan work to one's advantage. A year ago my current family and I decided to sell our home in Southern California because we wanted to semi-retire. After several months of looking for a new home we decided to move to Texas where the housing market seems to still be affordable and bought a beautiful brand new home on 1.2 acres of land having an asking price of $320,000.00. After a lot of negotiating, I ended up with a sale price of $255,000.00. I decided to make a down payment of $155,000.00, and wanted to finance the balance of $100,000 with an option loan because I wanted the advantage of a low payment based on the note rate. I applied to World Savings and Loan for our home loan and asked for the option loan that used the Eleventh-District-Cost-of-Funds-Index, and was informed by the bank that they currently are not using this particular loan program. However, they offered me the COSI or the CODI option loans and after viewing the two option loans I decided on the CODI option loan as its history of movement was similar to that of the Eleventh-District-Cost-of-Funds-Index.

Once the loan was approved, we moved to Texas and began buying all new furniture, appliances and everything else we wanted, and needed for our new home. After about 45 days or so, the first mortgage payment came in, and upon opening the statement I noticed that the initial monthly payment was not what I had originally agreed to, so I called the bank. The bank informed me that there had been an upward move in the index, and hence the increase in the mortgage payment. I had calculated our monthly mortgage payment to be approximately $598.00.00 per month and the bank statement indicated the mortgage payment to be almost $798.00. Therefore, I wrote a check for the monthly mortgage payment and I also sent another check for $50,000.00 indicating the amount was to be applied directly to a principal reduction. Having calculated my new monthly mortgage payment to be approximately $345.00.00, based on the principal reduction, the next month's mortgage payment came in at $345.50, or fifty cents more than I had figured. Furthermore, I was able to determine the amount of principal reduction I wanted, when I wanted it, as in advantage thirteen. I also reduced the amount of profit the bank would now be able to make on my option loan as indicated in advantage fifteen, and increased the equity buildup in my home, as in advantage sixteen of the option loan.

Nevertheless, readers should now be able to understand how they can manipulate the option loan to their advantage whenever they decide to work the loan. Furthermore, I intend to wait until I recuperate the major expenditures I made to completely furnish my new home before I again start making additional monthly principal reductions. I will continue to make these principal reduction payments until I get a monthly mortgage payment of below $100.00 per month, thereby allowing the bank to make all the remaining interest they can, by law, on my home loan. Currently, as previously mentioned in this book, my monthly principal and interest (PI) payment is now $35.00. Note: Should the reader be wondering how I go about negotiating such great deals, don't get too disappointed as I have included a separate and complete "Bonus" section on "How to Negotiate on Anything" at the end of the book.

Loan Broker vs. Mortgage Banker vs. Direct Lender

Let's start with the loan broker vs. the mortgage banker. Basically, both of these lenders are the same, in that they both have access to virtually any major federal or state chartered lending institutions. However, the versatility advantage to homebuyers belongs to the mortgage broker as opposed to the mortgage banker. The reason for this is that the mortgage broker is under no responsibility whatsoever to meet any certain funding dollar requirements with any lender that he or she may be doing business with, as opposed to the mortgage banker, who has to maintain a relationship commitment with his or her direct funding associates, whom he or she agrees to fund home loans through.

Allow me to explain this situation so that everyone will be able to understand the difference between the mortgage broker and the mortgage banker. To receive designation as a mortgage banker, the company must produce certain evidence that the mortgage banker is financially stable and normally registered with the Securities and Exchange Commission (SEC) so that he/she may sell homebuyers loans in the secondary market. However, it is not necessary for all mortgage bankers to be registered with the SEC in order to receive a direct line of credit from a major lender or investment firm for mortgage-lending purposes. Moreover, because of the strict requirements that are necessary to receive the designation of mortgage banker, the mortgage banker will seek a major lender or investment firm for an exclusive mortgage-funding dollar-amount approval, and make a commitment to funnel home loans through the major lender or investment firm each and every month in order to meet funding requirements.

Looking at this process from another point of view, a mortgage banker makes an agreement and commitment to their major lender or investment firm to submit home loans in the amount of 5 million, 10 million, 15 million, 20 million, or more dollars' worth of mortgage-loan business each and every month in order for the mortgage banker to maintain a direct line of credit, or what the mortgage bankers refer to as portfolio loans. Remember, a portfolio loan means that the lender will fund, maintain, and service the homebuyer's home loan. These loans are also referred to as in-house loans or shelf loans.

I am going to elucidate on this a little further so that prospective homebuyers fully understand what could happen to them should they decide to use a mortgage banker for their home loan. Let's say a mortgage banker has a funding commitment to their major lending source to submit and fund 10 million dollars a month in mortgage loans in order for them to maintain their funding line of credit. In a prospective homebuyer's opinion, where do you think your home loan will be submitted to first by a mortgage banker? What kind of interest rate will homebuyers be subjected to from the mortgage banker's major lending source? What kind of origination points will homebuyers be subjected to by the mortgage banker who has to channel their home loan through his/her major lending source in order to maintain their mortgage funding line of credit? I could go on and on with questions like these, but I believe that homebuyers will be able to come to their own conclusions.

Let's now examine the mortgage broker vs. the direct lender, but first, we want the homebuyers to understand that a mortgage broker may or may not seek a direct lender when it comes time to submit their home loan for a loan funding commitment and approval. The reason is that the mortgage broker may be able to find the homebuyers a better interest rate for less money from their other lending sources. However, if a homebuyer feels more secure with a direct lending source, then the mortgage broker will be more than happy to submit the home loan to the lending institution of the homebuyer's choice at a considerable savings. The reason for the savings to homebuyers is that the mortgage broker can "buy" the same identical loan from a direct lender at a wholesale price and pass the savings to the homebuyers.

Great, this sounds wonderful, but what is the advantage to homebuyers of using a mortgage broker vs. a direct lender? Versatility! In the event that the mortgage broker encounters any problems concerning homebuyers, e.g., poor credit, lack of sufficient income, judgments, lack of verification of down payment funds, etc., the mortgage broker can repackage the homebuyers' home loan information and resubmit their loan package as many times as necessary to other lenders seeking a commitment and funding approval, and the mortgage broker will not make any additional demands on homebuyers for more monies.

Nevertheless, in the event that homebuyers are turned down for a home loan by a direct lender, they will have to start all over again, and they will have to pay for another credit and appraisal report, as the direct lending banks are not required to give their home-buying clients their credit and appraisal reports, or even copies of them. Likewise, as homebuyers can see, this could become a very expensive process, and unfortunately, this has been going on for some time, all to the detriment of the home-buying public as well as the real-estate industry.

Let's look at an example of the versatility that a mortgage broker can offer to prospective homebuyers. Years ago I had to submit a homebuyer's home loan application to several different lenders before receiving a home loan funding commitment for them. However, even though getting homebuyers a home loan funding commitment was a consideration to me, it was not my only major consideration, as I knew that I would eventually be able to find a lender who would fund my client's home loan. My major concern was keeping my client from having to spend any more hard-earned money in order for me to find him a home loan. Furthermore, had this homebuyer been dealing with me when I was with a direct lender banking institution, their home loan would have been turned down. Likewise, had my clients decided to use another direct lender instead of a mortgage broker, they would have spent in excess of $2,800.00 just for the credit and appraisal reports. However, as a mortgage broker, I only had to charge my clients $350.00 for their credit and appraisal reports as a one-time fee, and yet I submitted and resubmitted these clients home loan application file to seven different lenders before I finally got them a funding commitment for their home.

The bottom line for homebuyers, is that their determination to choose a mortgage broker, a mortgage banker, or a direct lender should be based upon the homebuyer's knowledge of their financial capability and personal credit history, as well as his/her spouse's credit history. As to which lenders homebuyers will select, this will be up to the homebuyers to decide, and it depends upon the homebuyer's understanding of the above information.

As the reader can see, the advantage of having a mortgage broker seems to be overwhelming, as mortgage brokers do not have any funding commitments to meet or satisfy. On the other hand, mortgage bankers may also provide homebuyers with the versatility they may require after the mortgage bankers have satisfied their contractual commitment to their direct lending source. As for the direct lenders, well, this choice will have to be left up to the homebuyer's own good judgment, as well as his/her knowledge of the financial mortgage home loan market.

Nevertheless, the advantage in the competition between the mortgage brokers vs. the mortgage banker goes to the mortgage broker. However, depending on the mortgage banker's ability to satisfy the loan funding requirements of his/her direct lending source, the mortgage banker should be able to offer homebuyers the same versatility that mortgage brokers can offer. Moreover, the question to the mortgage banker should be, what is the mortgage bankers funding requirements, and have they satisfied the loan funding requirement of their direct lending source?

In the contest between mortgage brokers and direct lenders, (savings-and-loan banks) the advantage definitely goes to the mortgage broker. Between mortgage bankers and direct lenders, the advantage goes to the mortgage bankers. Direct lenders, as a rule, have notably higher interest rates and fees than the mortgage brokers and mortgage bankers. As to why this is the situation with the direct lenders, no one knows, and no one that I know in the loan industry was able to offer an adequate explanation over the years I have spent in the mortgage loan business.

What Is Bait-and-Switch, and Does It Apply to the Lending Industry?

Bait and switch is nothing more than a mortgage loan consultant, loan officer, or lender quoting homebuyers an interest rate figure and loan points that do not exist, in anticipation of receiving an unsuspecting homebuyer's mortgage loan application. To answer the next question, which is, does bait and switch apply to the lending industry? I must state, even though I don't want to, that I am sorry and sad to say that it does. It is called low-balling, hanging carrots, or teaser-rate quoting.

In the loan industry, the professionals call it entrapment. In other words, the mortgage loan consultant, loan officer, or lender who tells the best story to homebuyers by low-balling, hanging carrots, or quoting teaser rates usually, and unfortunately, wins homebuyer approval. Notice I said unfortunately, because homebuyers will definitely be the ones who will lose in this situation! And that is exactly what will happen to homebuyers that are subjected to the bait-and-switch process. Homebuyers will usually end up getting a mortgage loan that they don't understand, that will place them in a position of going into foreclosure or bankruptcy three, five, or seven years down the road.

Nevertheless, the bait-and-switch process was created in response to the tremendous competition between the various lending institutions and the mortgage loan consultants, and loan officers vying for mortgage finance business. Because of this intense competition, the mortgage loan consultants, and loan officers have forgone professionalism in anticipation of making the almighty dollar. Therefore, homebuyers need to beware of mortgage loan consultants and loan officers who may attempt to intimidate homebuyers into filling out a residential loan application during their first encounter. Remember, it is the homebuyer's hard-earned money that the mortgage loan consultants and loan officers are after. Should homebuyers feel intimidated, pressured or uncomfortable with the lenders, they should feel free to excuse the mortgage loan consultants or loan officers. Since it is the homebuyer's money, it therefore becomes the homebuyer's right to inform the mortgage loan consultants or loan officers that he/she will take their advice into consideration, and may get back to them after reviewing the financial information that they have presented.

One of my favorite techniques is to thank the mortgage loan consultants or loan officers for their time, and then inform them that I have two or more lenders to interview before I will be able to make a decision. This is when the true professional will emerge! Professional mortgage loan consultants or loan officers will not only agree with the homebuyers, but they will also encourage homebuyers to interview several other lenders. The amateur, or high-stress, mortgage loan consultants or loan officers will attempt to dissuade homebuyers from interviewing with other lenders, in an attempt to secure the homebuyers' signatures on the loan application while they are still with the homebuyers. Likewise, this is the time when the amateurs will low-ball, hang carrots, or offer teaser rates to homebuyers in anticipation of enticing them into performing now, by attempting to complete the residential loan application with the potential homebuyers.

Homebuyers should also realize that the mortgage loan consultants, and loan officers who attempt to intimidate or pressure homebuyers into performing, are, usually, new mortgage loan officers who have been in the mortgage loan business ninety days or less. However, I have also seen the technique of low-balling, hanging carrots, or offering teaser rates used by seasoned mortgage loan consultants, and it is usually done because they haven't made any commissions for a long period of time, and are under a lot of stress to make money. However, regardless of which type of mortgage loan consultants or loan officers homebuyers may encounter, if they attempt to resort to low-balling, hanging carrots, or offering teaser rates in order to get your mortgage loan business, homebuyers should feel free to dismiss them as soon as possible, and look someplace else for a home loan.

Professional real-estate mortgage loan consultants, loan officers, and lenders will ask (or should ask) homebuyers a lot of questions concerning wants, needs, and desires in relation to their home purchase. The professional should be kind, courteous, and knowledgeable. The professional should take all the time homebuyers require to explain, and answer any questions homebuyers may have concerning the various loan programs that homebuyers may inquire about. They should also be able to explain the ins and outs of these loan programs to the complete satisfaction of the homebuyers. The professional will advise homebuyers on the various types of documentation that they will be required to fill out and sign in order to start the home loan application. Moreover, professionals will take the necessary time to show and explain the forms in the residential loan application to homebuyers, and answer any questions to their satisfaction. The professional will trust homebuyers and may even give the residential loan application package to them to fill out at their convenience, knowing that homebuyers could submit the loan application to another lender.

The professional will maintain his/her faith and trust the homebuyers. The amateurs will continue to low-ball, hang carrots or offer teaser rates, as well as, attempt to intimidate and insist pressure the homebuyers to perform immediately. Again, I could go on and on, but remember, the professional real-estate mortgage loan consultants, loan officers, and lenders will have your best interest and concerns uppermost in their minds. The amateur, intimidating, high-pressure loan officers will have their bank account uppermost in their minds. Nevertheless, homebuyers need to be aware of the low-balling, carrot hanging, and teaser rates in the form of interest rates, and loan point figures that they may be quoted, because 99.99 percent of the time, homebuyers will pay dearly, just because they heard what they wanted to hear from a mortgage loan consultant, loan officer, or lender who told them the best story.

Let's look at an example of an actual low-balling, carrot-hanging, and teaser-rate-offering loan quote scenario. Let's say the Federal Reserve Board, that plays the major role in the United States' mortgage-interest-rate quoting structure, quotes interest rates at a particular figure on any given day to the lending community. The FNMA and the FHLMC will pick up this information and then report the current conforming fixed interest rates at a given figure to the lending institutions. The lending institutions then establish, and quote their interest rates with a corresponding buy-rate point structure to the mortgage-loan market.

Now, let's say that the current fixed interest rate for a conforming mortgage loan is being quoted at 7.500 percent at two points, including the buy rate by one lender, and another lender is quoting homebuyers 7.000 percent at two points. Homebuyers would be wise to immediately question the lender, concerning the quote with the lower interest rate, and unless this lender knows of another Federal Reserve Board, FNMA, or FHLMC somewhere in the world other than the United States, homebuyers would be getting lured into a bait-and-switch situation. In other words, should there be a variance greater than .125 percent below the current market rate being quoted at two points or less, homebuyers need to question the mortgage loan consultant or loan officer as to how their lender will be able to perform. It may be possible for the lender to offer the potential homebuyers the lower interest rate at 2 points as indicated above, providing the lender is going to assist the homebuyers with buying down the interest rate. However, this is highly unlikely to occur, as the lenders are not in the business of subsidizing homebuyers who are applying for a home loan. So what will the real cost to homebuyers be to buy the interest rate down? As I indicated before, it is the homebuyers money that the lenders are after; therefore, homebuyers should not hesitate to get rid of a mortgage loan consultant, loan officer, or lender if they think they are being low-balled or given a teaser rate just to get their mortgage loan business. On the other hand, the lower interest-rate quote may be legitimate, but I can guarantee the prospective homebuyers that the loan program will not be the same conforming loan program being quoted by the first lender.

If homebuyers find themselves getting caught up in a bait-and-switch situation and the mortgage loan consultant, loan officer, or lender was recommended by a real-estate agent, then the homebuyer needs to inform the real-estate agent that he/she did not care for the mortgage loan consultant, loan officer, or lender, and the reason should be given to the real-estate agent. Should the real-estate agent question the homebuyer about their decision, the homebuyer needs to stand his/her ground, and not be pushed around by a real-estate agent. Remember, it is the homebuyer's money that is at stake, and the real-estate agent's job is to assist homebuyers with the purchase and closing of their home loans. Homebuyers need to feel free to ask the real-estate agent for another mortgage loan consultant, loan officer, or lender referral and/or inform the real-estate agent that they will seek out their own lending source. Likewise, never be intimidated by a real-estate agent, mortgage loan consultant, loan officer, or lender, as they get paid only if they satisfy homebuyers' mortgage loan needs! Furthermore, homebuyers should feel free to get rid of any of these people in the event that homebuyers feel that they are being pressured or intimidated into purchasing while applying for a home loan. Moreover, should any one of these people get out of line when doing business with homebuyers, homebuyers can request to speak with the real-estate office broker or the lender's broker, and if homebuyers are still not satisfied, they can report any or all of these real-estate licensed persons and personnel to the Department of Real Estate, and request a complaint form and file for monetary compensation.

Unfortunately, there are a lot of bait-and-switch techniques being used in the mortgage loan marketplace to get the homebuyers' money, but the bottom line is always the same. Homebuyers will always lose if they buy into the best story, or the story that they want to hear. The most commonly used bait-and switch technique used, is when homebuyers call, or are called by a mortgage loan consultant, loan officer, or lender for an interest-rate and point quote. This is the time when the loan consultant, loan officer, or lender will attempt quoting homebuyers very low interest rates, as well as, very low-point structures, or the point-fee structure for their home loan. Moreover, the mortgage loan consultant, loan officer, or lender may even offer to lock in an interest rate and point quote for thirty, forty-five, or even sixty days, or until homebuyers receive a loan commitment. In fact, the lenders may even give homebuyers the interest rate and point lock-in in written form, that will not be worth the paper it is written on, in anticipation of locking in the homebuyers to keep them from looking for or checking other interest rates, and loan costs with other lenders.

To put this in its proper perspective, let me say, that anyone, including homebuyers, can lock in an interest rate and point cost until loan commitment, because until a homebuyer's loan is approved, and a funding commitment has been issued, homebuyers have a piece of paper worth absolutely nothing! As a rule, fixed interest rates cannot be locked in until the homebuyer's loan has been approved. However, an exception to this rule can occur, but only at the prevailing real interest rate and points that are available, then, and only then, can the rates and points be locked in until the homebuyer's loan is funded. Big difference!

Moving on, let's say that a pair of homebuyers are approaching a closing date, and on the last day or so they receive a call from the mortgage loan consultant, loan officer, or lender, and the lender states: "Congratulations, Mr. And Mrs. Homebuyers, your new home loan has been approved, but the best prevailing interest rate is 9 percent instead of the 7.5 percent that was quoted, and the cost for the loan will be 2.5 points." This tactic is the bait-and-switch technique being used in its finest hour. However, besides the fact that homebuyers may become extremely upset (to say the least) when this happens, they are left with three choices: (1) Accept the lender's terms, pay the price and close the escrow (this is most likely). (2) Refuse the loan and extend the escrow until the homebuyers can find an "honest" mortgage loan consultant, loan officer, or lender, and providing the sellers will agree to extend the escrow period, or (3) Force the lender by telling them to honor their original agreement, or you will report them to either the OTS or the OCC. Upon hearing this information, the lender will most likely agree to honor their original agreement, as they definitely do not want to be investigated or shut down by the OTS or OCC.

Furthermore, homebuyers had better hope that the sellers are not part of a domino sales effect in which three or more sellers are all selling at the same time, and all of them are relying on the final homebuyers to complete their home loan transaction. If homebuyers find themselves in this situation, I can guarantee them that they will become subjected to a tremendous amount of pressure by the real-estate agents and the lenders, who will attempt to force the sale. Homebuyers don't—I repeat, don't—submit to the pressure from these people. In fact, stand your ground, and inform all of them that you will be happy to turn them all over to the Department of Real Estate and the OTS or the OCC if they don't back off. Assuming the homebuyers stood their ground, and put everyone in their places, I can assure homebuyers that everything will be worked out between the real-estate agents and the lenders, in order to make the entire transaction beneficial to everyone involved in a domino home sales transaction. Incidentally, this is the time during which homebuyers will have the greatest amount of influence in the real-estate transaction. If I were involved, I would force the lender to give me an interest rate below the original quoted 7.500 percent, and have them reduce their points to 1.000 percent for causing me so much trouble.

When homebuyers talk to mortgage loan consultants, loan officers, or lenders and request an interest-rate and point quote, and the lenders start asking homebuyers a lot of direct questions concerning their wants, needs, and desires, homebuyers may have found an honest lender. In other words, when lenders are concerned about homebuyers' wants, needs, and desires, the lenders will not quote homebuyers an interest rate or point figures until they have all the facts concerning the purchase details. The professional lenders will offer homebuyers several different financial programs, and offer alternatives that can be customized to satisfy the homebuyers' wants, needs, and desires. Remember, the professional lenders will be up front with homebuyers and will not utilize, or incorporate bait-and-switch techniques when it is time for them to close their home loan. When professional lenders quote homebuyers an interest rate and point fees, they will honor their commitment to homebuyers regardless of the commission they would make, and regardless of any point-buy-rate increase incurred by the lender prior to funding a homebuyer's home loan, even though it would reduce the lender's commission.

Nevertheless, should homebuyers be fortunate enough to find a professional real-estate lender, the key that will let homebuyers know whether or not they are dealing with a professional is the lender's acknowledgement of homebuyers' wants, needs, and desires. The professional will be up front with homebuyers from the very beginning of the home loan transaction. The professional will be glad to share their knowledge with homebuyers, and will impart additional information when homebuyers request it, or when the professional believes it is necessary for homebuyers to understand a particular loan program. Find a professional that is concerned about homebuyers and their purchases, and you have found not only a professional lender, but also a new friend!

Note: This little insider tip will put a stop to any attempted bait-and-switch process by the lenders or their representatives. Homebuyers who think that they are getting involved in a bait-and-switch situation should request that the mortgage loan consultants, loan officers, or lenders involved, provide them with a good faith estimate (GFE) in the beginning of the loan process. By making this request, homebuyers will be forcing the lender to provide the real interest rates available, and in the event that the interest rates change by more than an eighth of a point, the lender is required to issue another GFE to homebuyers; this is true until their loan closes. This request will also put a stop to any so-called surprises that homebuyers may not be expecting at the time of their loan closing.

SECTION 4: DANGEROUS LOANS

Dangerous Mortgage Loans to Avoid

Basically, other than the standard thirty-year and fifteen-year-fixed-interest-rate loan programs, all the other available mortgage-interest-rate loans can be classified as being dangerous loans, especially, if homebuyers do not understand how these other loan programs function. However, there are a few mortgage-interest-rate loan programs that are outright dangerous for all unsuspecting homebuyers. Currently, the most dangerous loan program in the marketplace is known as, and disguised as a home equity line of credit known as the HELOC loan. This particular loan program is tied to the prime rate, has a margin from 3.500 percent to 4.500 percent plus a line margin—the three-year Treasury index—that is then added to the margin, and it also has a very, very quiet life cap of 18 percent, that in my professional opinion should be against the law when attached and recorded against a homeowner's real property. Boys and girls, this HELOC loan can put you into bankruptcy so fast that you won't have time to blink.

The HELOC is nothing more than a line of credit, but when one takes the time to analyze this loan, he/she will find out the following information: The index is added to the margin, and based on current calculations, the effective interest rate would be anywhere from 8.125 percent to 9.125 percent, and now the lenders add the line margin, that could be anywhere from 3 percent to 9.125 percent. Homebuyers with this type of loan have a monthly payment ranging anywhere from the low end of 11.125 percent to 12.125 percent, and 12.125 percent to 13.125 percent on the high end. Note that the lenders who are currently offering the HELOC loans have not incorporated the use of the line margin as an add on that would effect the overall interest rate of this loan; however, the line margin add on is indicated in the lender's rate sheets, which means it gives the lender the right to use and include the line margin should the lender decide to make more money with the HELOC loan. Furthermore, homebuyers also have to contend with the life cap of 18 percent, making the HELOC loan the most dangerous mortgage loan in the marketplace. Incidentally, homebuyers who are not aware of how a line of credit works need to pay attention to the following information.

A line of credit, whether it is being offered by a banking institution, a lender, or even a credit card company is nothing more than money on the sidelines for homeowners to have access to in the event that they need additional monies for whatever reason. However, other than the initial up-front fees that may be required for obtaining the line of credit, the line of credit will not normally cost homeowners anything until they make a withdrawal from the line of credit. This is when the banking institutions, lenders, or credit card companies start drooling, because they are about to start making a tremendous amount of money from the homeowners' line of credit. Note: Some lenders may require the homeowners to withdraw the entire amount of their line of credit all at once. Caution: No one should ever agree to accept this kind of a line of credit!

Moreover, once the homeowners activate their line of credit, it is automatically recorded as a second mortgage loan against the homeowner's home. Therefore, homeowners and prospective homebuyers should avoid seeking any sort of line of credit whatsoever, as these credit lines will be recorded against their homes, and will be very expensive loans.

Likewise, I highly suggest that everyone avoid the HELOC loan at all costs! Moreover, unlike some lines of credit, the HELOC loan is recorded as a second mortgage loan as soon as escrow closes without the homeowners having made any withdraws. Nevertheless, should homeowners or homebuyers decide that they would like to have extra monies, and they have enough equity in their homes, then they should apply for a second mortgage, as these are much safer loans that are also fully amortized at fixed interest rates that can be a 30/15 conversion loan or a balloon payment loan, but be sure to check with the lender, and/or a 30/30 fully amortized loan, as well as, interest-only loans.

Another mortgage loan which I also classify as being dangerous, is the option loan, which has recently been given a makeover by certain lenders in the United States that can now make the option loan an extremely dangerous mortgage loan. Here is how it works: The lenders have decided to take the best mortgage loan in the marketplace known as the adjustable negative loan or option loan, and are using a 1.10 percent, 1.15 percent, or 1.20 percent maximum-deferred-interest add-on, or wrap-around, that in turn shortens the amount of time before the loan has to be re-amortized, and takes away some of the major advantages of the option loan. By shortening the re-amortization time factor to 1.10 percent, 1.15 percent, or 1.20 percent maximum-deferred-interest add-on, or wrap-around, means that a homebuyer will only have between three or four years before this loan will take a major jump in monthly mortgage payments. Basically, the loan functions the same as a regular option loan in the first three or four years, but because of the limited amount of deferred interest being allowed to accumulate before the loan has to recast, the shorter the time period homebuyers or homeowners will have to take the ancillary advantages the option loan program offers.

In other words, as a result of shortening the time factor for the maximum allowable deferred interest, the loan does not give homebuyers or homeowners the overall protection that the standard option loan can offer. As an example, let's say a homebuyer is offered a start rate of 1.25 percent, and a note rate of 7.75 percent, how long will it take for this loan to reach a maximum of 1.10 percent wrap-around of the deferred? In this scenario it will take less than three years, and at that time the monthly mortgage payment will almost double. Let's look at an example using a $400,000.00 loan amount, and see what happens in less than thirty-six months. Using the 1.25 percent start rate, homeowners have a monthly mortgage interest payment of $1,333.00 in year one, and using the standard 7.5 percent annual payment cap, the second year payment would be $1,433.00, and year three would be $1,540.00. Likewise, using the 7.75 percent note rate, that the homeowners should be paying, in order to make their monthly principal-and-interest mortgage payments, would now be approximately $2,866.00.

Now, assuming that the homeowners decided not to work the loan to their advantage and they instead allowed the deferred interest to wrap around to their mortgage, let's see what happens to the time factor in order to accumulate a maximum 1.10 percent wrap-around of the deferred interest. If we take the above monthly mortgage payments and subtract them from the required monthly mortgage payments, and multiply each year's figures by twelve, we would have the following approximate rounded annual deferred interest figures of: $18,392.00, $17,192.00, and $15,902.00 for years one, two, and three, respectively. Now we simply add up these three figures, and we get $51,486.00 of deferred interest that would be allowed to wrap around to the homeowners' mortgage loan. However, if you remember, the maximum allowable wrap-around of deferred interest with this loan program was

1.10 percent for a total of $40,000.00. So what happens to the homeowners' loan? When the 1.10 percent or $40,000.00 loan amount has been reached, the loan is re-amortized, or recast, and converted to the monthly note-rate mortgage payment of $2,866.00, thereby almost doubling the homeowner's monthly mortgage loan payment in less than three years.

The reader can now see why it is extremely important to understand the inner workings of mortgage loan programs being marketed to homebuyers and homeowners by lenders. Furthermore, any negative, or option loan that has monthly mortgage payment term shorter than five years, allowing a maximum of 1.25 percent wrap-around of deferred interest, needs to be avoided at all costs by homebuyers and homeowners, because there would be insufficient time to allow homebuyers and homeowners to work the advantages of the option loan, and at the same time drive the banks crazy!

Other dangerous mortgage loans to be on the lookout for would include the 2/28 and 3/27, also known as Band-Aid loans, that were discussed earlier, and are normally used for low income potential homebuyers who have a history of bad credit. The only thing to remember about these loan programs is that they will give homebuyers sufficient time to clear up their credit and get into an A-paper loans as soon as possible. The other dangerous loans, known as the 5/25, 7/23, and 3/27 loan programs, should be approached with extreme caution. These loans can be good loans for homebuyers who intend to sell and move on again in three, five, or seven years, but make sure you fully understand what these loan programs will convert to along with a complete understanding of the new conversion loans, in the event homebuyers do not sell their home before the expiration period is up.

In recent years, I have seen the inauguration of mortgage loans known as interest-only loans covering five and ten year periods of time. Technically, there is nothing wrong with these mortgage loans, as they offer homebuyers the ability to purchase higher-end properties without any risk, and not having to concern themselves with making any principal payments. However, unless homebuyers are in a very high tax bracket, and need the interest-only mortgage payments as a pure tax write-off, or they are willing to concentrate on making principal-reduction payments on a regular basis, or they plan to live in their home for only 5 or 10 years before relocating, there is little chance that they would benefit from these mortgage loan programs. Otherwise, homeowners would only be able to rely on any appreciation that may take place during the term of these loan programs, in order to benefit from their home purchase in the form of some equity build up in their the home.

Furthermore, homebuyers also need to realize that these interest only loans can backfire on you should the home market take a downward turn. As an example, I will use one of my neighbors who moved into our newly developed neighborhood about six or seven months after we moved into our new home. Let's call him Ben. When Ben moved into his new custom built home next door to us, it took about a year and half or so before we became good friends. Ben was an easy going guy that technically did not have the financial capability to move into our neighborhood, let alone be able to afford making principal and interest payments on his newly constructed home. Nevertheless, and even though we did not know it at the time, Ben was able to finance his home with an interest only loan for five years from the proceeds that he received from the sale of his home in Arlington, Texas. Everything seemed to be fine until Ben started approaching the fifth year on his interest only loan when he approached me, and asked if I knew anyone in the mortgage loan industry? Asking Ben why he wanted to know, Ben explained to me that he had an interest only loan that was coming due, and that he could not afford both the principal and interest payment on his home. When I asked Ben what he had built his home for, he stated that it cost him $350,000.00 to build, and he was able to make a down payment of $70,000.00 with a bridge loan until his other home sold. However, Ben only received $84,000.00 from the sale of his other home, and putting down the $70,000.00 plus fees, only left Ben a little less than $10,000.00 from the real estate transaction. Okay, Ben now has a $280,000.00 mortgage balance that would cost him approximately $1751.00 per month in PI payments alone, not including taxes and insurance that Ben could not afford to pay. Therefore, Ben opted for an interest only loan, and since Ben did not know what his effective interest rate was, I can only guess, and figured his interest to be somewhere around the high 5 percent range to the low six percent range. Likewise, Ben indicated his monthly interest payment to be a little over $1100.00 per month, whereas his total PITI payment would have been around $2100.00 to $2300.00 per month. However, the housing market, as everyone knows, was making major downward movements, and Ben's home value went upside down to the point that Ben was unable to refinance his home. Therefore, in order to stop any possible foreclosure proceedings, I advised Ben that his only way out was to sell his home and salvage what he could and save his credit. Ben listed and sold his new home within two days, and was able to get out of trouble. We then advised Ben not to get another interest only loan and he agreed. Furthermore, we suggested to Ben that he should buy another home, only this time, something that he would be able to afford. Apparently, everything has turned out okay for Ben, and every now and then we occasionally see him driving around with a smile on his face. The reason for pointing out Ben's situation is that this incident occurs more often than not, as potential homebuyers usually want more than they can afford, and find themselves in trouble somewhere down the road because they did not take the time to understand their mortgage loan limits and limitations, and what could take place in the housing market.

Likewise, and as ironic as it may sound, interest-only loans are dangerous loans for the lenders. Why? Because interest-only homebuyers have very little to lose if something goes wrong. In the event that they cannot make their monthly interest-only mortgage payments, they just simply walk away from their home, and let the lenders take the loss. If one were to think about it, an interest-only loan would be a good way to go, especially, in the reverse-mortgage market, in which housing prices go upside down, or in the event of an economic slowdown that has an effect on a homebuyer's ability to sell a home. Homebuyers could simply walk away from these loan programs without suffering any major setbacks except for a foreclosure that would show up on their credit report. However, even though these homebuyers would have a foreclosure recorded on their credit report, and even though the foreclosure remains on their credit report for seven to ten years, these same homebuyers could go out and purchase another home twelve months later, with the only provision being that they would have to accept a 2/28 or 3/27 mortgage loan. So who cares? The lenders of interest-only loan programs should care!

Another dangerous loan program that the lenders have managed to come up with recently in an attempt to screw up the option loan is just the result of another twisted thought process whereby the lenders believe that they can fool homebuyers by enticing them with a variation on the option loan. Lenders have decided to offer the basic option loan to prospective homebuyers, but the loan now includes the following twist: The lenders are allowing homebuyers to have a five-year fixed-interest payment based on a low start rate of 2.500 percent, and having a note rate of 7.500 percent. However, what the lenders haven't taken into consideration is the fact, that if the homebuyers work the loan according to the section entitled "The Loan You Can Drive like Your Own Car," homebuyers can defeat the lenders at their own game by knocking down the principal balance while still making small monthly mortgage interest payments over the next five years. Therefore, at the end of the five-year interest-only payment period, the lender will re-amortize this loan only to find out that the loan program did not make the kind of monies that the lenders thought they would make, because the homebuyers took advantage of the loan program, and reduced the principal sufficiently enough to take the lender's profit out of the loan.

Caution: Understanding how this loan program works is very important, because if homebuyers do not work down the principal balance, the lender will be allowed to wrap around a considerable amount of deferred interest that will be added back to the original loan amount at the end of the five-year fixed-interest-rate period. When the loan reaches the 1.10 percent, 1.15 percent, 1.20 percent, or 1.25 percent period, the loan will be re-amortized. Note: The 1.10 percent maximum wrap-around of deferred interest will recast in less than three and one-half years, assuming homebuyers make the minimum monthly mortgage loan payment.

For example, using a $400,000 loan amount and the 2.500 percent start rate figure, homebuyers would have a monthly mortgage loan payment of approximately $1,580.00 for the next five years. However, homebuyers should be making the note rate monthly mortgage payment of $2,797.00 in order to cover the principal-and-interest payments over the same period of time. Again, we simply subtract the difference, and this time we get a figure of $1,217.00. This should be applied to the deferred interest. Next we multiply this figure by twelve and get a figure of $14,604.00 in deferred annual interest. We then multiply by five (for five years) and we get a figure of $73,020.00 of total deferred interest that would wrap around to the original loan amount of $400,000. When re-amortized by the lenders, a homebuyer's new monthly mortgage payment would be based on a loan amount of $473,020.

Nevertheless, the only two dangerous aspects of this loan program that I can see are the facts that: (1) This loan does not allow for a closure between the start rate and the note rate, and as long as there is no closure between the start rate and the note rate, homebuyers will be subjected to the large spread between the two, and will continue to incur the deferred interest, and (2) in the event that interest rates continue to rise, the deferred interest spread will continue to increase, based on the particular index that the lenders are using for the loan program. Therefore, assuming homebuyers do not work this loan to their advantage, the lenders are guaranteed to make a lot of money on these hybrid loan programs.

As the reader can now see, the lending institutions will continue to screw up various mortgage loan programs in anticipation of cheating homebuyers out of more and more of their hard-earned monies, if they believe that they can get away with it. However, I believe that homebuyers and homeowners throughout the United States should have a level playing field with the giant financial institutions that are all vying for the almighty dollar in the mortgage loan industry, hence, the reason for this book. Nevertheless, the bottom line for any homebuyers or homeowners is to remember, when considering any home loan program, make sure he/she completely understands the proposed loan in its entirety before signing any loan documentation. This is especially critical when viewing any loan program that will convert to some other loan program sometime in the future. In other words, if homebuyers don't understand all the complexities or inner workings of a loan program, as well as, what the loan program will become in the future, they should not accept the loan!

Dangerous Margins/Spreads

As the reader should already know, margins are the fixed aspects of adjustable loan programs, as well as, the profit to the portfolio lenders servicing these loans. Back in the early 1980s, the majority of margins were running between 1.50 percent and 2.00 percent, depending on the creditworthiness of homebuyers. However, as time went by, the portfolio lenders started to realize the additional monthly profit potential they would receive by increasing the margins. Therefore, the portfolio lenders started slowly moving the margins up, taking them to 2.25 percent, 2.50 percent, and 2.625 percent, etc. Now there are margins as high as 4.99 percent, which in my professional opinion should be against the law, and anything over 3.00 percent in a margin should be classified as predatory lending! Furthermore, there is no reason for the lenders to be allowed to continue to take advantage of the home-buying public by increasing the margins on adjustable loan programs, as the lenders are already making a tremendous amount of monies on these loans.

In my professional opinion, margins that are in excess of 3.00 percent should be addressed by the OTS or the OCC, as excess margins are outright dangerous because their only purpose is to make more money for the portfolio lenders at the expense of the home-buying public. If you are homebuyers that are looking for an adjustable loan program, and you get quoted a margin in excess of 3.00 percent, find another lender! If the margin is close to 3.00 percent, such as 3.125 percent or 3.25 percent, etc., seriously consider buying down the margin to 2.50 percent, 2.75 percent, or even 2.95 percent, if you have the extra money, consider a margin buy-down. By buying down the margins, homebuyers will be lowering their overall monthly mortgage interest rate payments, which will place homebuyers in a better position, in the event they have to or decide to make the start rate interest only payment instead of the note rate principal-and-interest payment. Remember, homebuyers have the right to move back and forth between the start rate, and note rate monthly mortgage payments throughout the term of the option loan.

Dangerous Indexes to Avoid

Back in the early 1980s, the only index that was being used with the option loan was the Eleventh District Cost of Funds (11th DCOF). The 11th DCOF was primarily used on the West Coast and was, and still is, determined by all the monies being deposited into and going out of savings accounts, checking accounts, six-month and one-year CDs, gold, silver, bonds, etc., through the major banking institutions located in

California, Arizona, and Nevada, which is located in the Eleventh Federal Reserve District of the United States, hence the name 11th DCOF. Incidentally, even to this day, the 11th DCOF is still the most stable of all of the indexes in the entire mortgage loan marketplace if you can find an adjustable loan using this index. During the early 1980s, interest rates skyrocketed up to as high as 23 percent, and all of the indexes, except the 11th DCOF, which barely broke the 12% mark, went over the 20 percent interest-rate mark.

Furthermore, it was during this period of time that people literally walked away from their homes, and left the state of California because there were no upper interest-rate limit guidelines in the form of life caps in those days to prevent homebuyers' mortgage loans from going through the roof, so to speak. In other words, in one month homebuyers were paying $800.00 a month in mortgage payments, and the next month they had to make a $1,200.00 payment, and in the next couple of months they had to make $1,800.00 monthly payments. This went on until homebuyers could no longer afford to live in their homes. Bankruptcies ran rampant across the United States, credit was destroyed, and the overall economy was a disaster, similar to what our economy is now in 2015. Likewise, interest rates continued to fluctuate until finally, in the late 1980s, the interest rates once again came back down to a fairly reasonable mortgage lending rate range that was between 8.500 percent and 10.500 percent, where they remained until the early 1990s.

In the early 1990s, we entered a period of the lowest interest rates in the history of the United States since the period during the late 1940s and the late 1950s. Mortgage loan interest rates remained extremely low from the early 1990s until the early years of 2000. Nevertheless, all good things come to an end, and we are now seeing mortgage interest rates rising once again, and where they will eventually taper off is anyone's guess. However, because of this major debacle, which was caused by excessive inflation and a myriad of other circumstances, the Federal Home Loan Bank Board had to step in and force the mortgage lenders to place maximum life caps on all adjustable mortgage loans to prevent this situation from ever happening again in the home loan marketplace. Since then, the Federal Home Loan Bank Board, that was supposed to govern banking and the savings-and-loan associations, was abandoned and replaced by the Office of Thrift Supervision, also known as the OTS. Furthermore, and as mentioned earlier, our lustrous government has established another bank lending govern entity known as the Office of the Comptroller of Currency or OCC. However, in my opinion, the OTS is far more knowledgeable and capable than the OCC, as I have had the pleasure of dealing with the OTS, and the unfortunate encounter with the OCC, whose personnel did not seem to know what they are doing. Moreover, and as of this writing, concerning the lowest interest rates in the history of the United States that occurred in the 40's and 50's previously mentioned, mortgage interest rates have now gone even lower as of 2015. This has now established a new record low for mortgage interest rates in the history of the United States. Whether this is good or bad, only time will tell, but if one is old enough to remember, the same exact thing happened to Japan over a couple of decades ago, and to this day, Japan has never recovered or managed to increase their interest rates, so what is in store of the United States? Only time will tell.

Okay, so much for the history lesson. Getting back to the dangerous indexes to avoid, it wasn't until 1989 that the lending industry started coming up with a myriad of different indexes to be used in conjunction with the option loan program. Fortunately, the majority of these indexes have vanished from the mortgage marketplace because the majority of them did not seem to be acceptable to homebuyers for unknown reasons, or maybe homebuyers just simply didn't care for the acronyms. Nevertheless, let's look at some of the indexes that are currently being used in the mortgage-loan market for the option loan, and then I will point out the dangerous indexes that homebuyers should avoid.

Some of the current indexes being used with the option loan are the 11th DCOF Certificate of Deposit Index, which is used by World Savings and Loan in California, which was recently bought by Wachovia Bank N.A. that will also be offering the same option loans that had been offered by World Savings and Loan. These option loans are known as CODI and are calculated using the three-month Certificate of Deposit. Next is the Cost of Savings Index, which is also a Wachovia product known as COSI. This is calculated using the weighted average-cost-of-savings ratio, which is arrived at by dividing the annualized interest by the bank's total deposits on the last day of the month, multiplying by one hundred, and displaying the result as a percentage figure. However, the reader needs to know that Wachovia Bank N.A. was bought out by the Wells Fargo Bank, and we currently do not know the type of mortgage loans the Wells Fargo Bank has to offer potential homebuyers, other than the standard boring 30 and 15 year fixed rate loan programs. Moving on, we have the London Inter Bank Offer Rate (known as LIBOR), and the Monthly Treasury Average (known as MTA), that can be calculated using any of the following: one-month MTA, three-month MTA, the six-month MTA or the one-year MTA. If homebuyers are considering an MTA index with the option loan, they need to know which MTA index will be applied to calculate their note rate. However, before accepting any MTA index, I highly suggest that homebuyers review the history of the MTA for the last ten to twenty years in order to understand its stability in the mortgage loan marketplace. Information concerning the stability of the MTA is usually available from the lenders or via the internet.

Out of all of the aforementioned indexes, the one that I highly recommend that every homebuyer avoid is the LIBOR index. The reason for my recommendation is that the United States maintains absolutely no control over the LIBOR index, as this index is a European index. However, because the LIBOR index is a very lucrative moneymaking index for the banking institutions, it is widely used here in the United States. The LIBOR index is the most unstable of all the indexes used in the mortgage marketplace, and the index has been known to make major increases long before any of the other indexes. Next we have the MTA index, which homebuyers should also avoid if they are considering the option loan program. In fact, the only indexes that should even be considered when homebuyers are seeking a option loan program are: (1) The 11th DCOF, as history has proven this index to be the most stable of all of the indexes, and (2) Either the CODI or the COSI, as these indexes also maintain a track record of stable movement similar to that of the 11th DCOF, even though these indexes are, and have been a little higher in their overall monthly and annual adjustments over the years as compared with the 11th DCOF.

There are several additional indexes that are being used in the mortgage marketplace, primarily with the no negative, or payment shock loan programs. These are known as the six-month, one-year, three-year, five-year, seven-year, and ten-year Treasury indexes. Also used are the one-year, three-year, five-year, seven-year, and ten-year LIBOR indexes. However, the point that I would like to make to homebuyers is that unless they fully understand the implications, and inner workings of any of these no negative, or payment shock loan programs and their indexes, then I highly suggest that they avoid these loan programs at all costs. In fact, no one should get involved with a no negative, or payment shock loan program period. If homebuyers know that they will be selling their home in two to three years, then they should take a 5/25 or a 25/5 loan program. If homebuyers are going to move in three to five years, then they should look at a 7/23 or 23/7 loan program, as these loan programs will be far superior to any adjustable no-negative, or payment shock loan programs, providing homebuyers sell their homes in their respective time periods. Furthermore, in my professional opinion, the use of the no-negative, or payment shock loan programs should be eliminated from the mortgage marketplace, as these adjustable loan programs no longer serve any purpose other than to make the lenders more money.

Because the mortgage loan industry is constantly changing, there will be more and more indexes that will surface, and disappear in attempts to extract more money from the unsuspecting home-buying public as time goes on. Therefore, the more information, knowledge, and understanding homebuyers can get concerning these new loan programs, the better off they will be when they come face to face with lenders. By all means, don't be afraid to ask questions concerning any loan program you do not fully understand. Likewise, even though the prime rate has never been used as a viable adjustable-interest-rate mortgage loan program, in the event that the lenders should decide to offer the prime rate as an adjustable loan index, the prime rate index should be avoided at all costs, the same as the LIBOR index, as the prime rate is as volatile as the current LIBOR index.

Dangerous Life Caps to Avoid

Life caps came into play after the downfall of the home market back in the 1980s. They were implemented as a means to protect the home-buying public from becoming subjected to outrageous interest-rate increases for those homebuyers who purchased their homes with adjustable mortgage loan programs. However, in my professional opinion, the life caps are beginning to get out of line, as there are apparently no guidelines in effect that would limit the ceiling of adjustable loan life caps by the lending institutions. In the HELOC loan program, I have seen life caps as high as 18 percent, which in my opinion is outrageous, but because the HELOC loan is supposed to be a line of credit, it is not classified as being a mortgage loan, even though the HELOC would be recorded against a person's home as a second mortgage.

In the adjustable mortgage loan market, we are seeing life caps from as low as 9.99 percent to the high end of 13.95 percent, and unfortunately, the home-buying public is accepting these life cap figures without giving them a second thought. Nevertheless, let's take a look at what homebuyers could become subjected to in the event mortgage interest rates go as high as their life caps will allow. Let's take an adjustable mortgage loan of $395,000.00 having a start rate of 3.500 percent, a note rate of 7.500 percent, and a life cap of 12.950 percent, and see what happens to the homebuyer's monthly mortgage payment should the mortgage market interest rates go the 15 percent.

Using the above figures, homebuyers would have a start rate monthly mortgage loan payment of $1,774.00, and a note rate Payment of $2,762.00. Now, let's say that the mortgage market interest rates start escalating upwards and hits the 15 percent mark. Because homebuyers would have a life cap of only 12.950 percent in this situation, their note rate payment would now be calculated at 12.950 percent for a monthly mortgage loan payment requirement of $4,354.00, which they should be making in the way of principal-and-interest payments. In the event that homebuyers were making the start rate payment of $1,774.00, they would be subjected to approximately $988.00 per month in deferred interest, but at the life cap interest rate, the homebuyers' deferred interest would jump to approximately $2,580.00 per month, assuming they were still making the start rate payment.

Moreover, if we go a little deeper into this loan, assuming homebuyers are making the note rate payment; those homebuyers would still be subjected to deferred interest because of the difference between the note rate, and the life cap interest rate figure that they should be paying. So now we have a monthly interest-rate deferment of approximately $1,774.00, which is the exact payment figure of the start rate. However, in this case, the note rate becomes the start rate at $2,762.00, and the note rate becomes $4,354.00, or the life cap interest-rate payment that homebuyers should be making in order to make monthly principal-and-interest mortgage loan payments. In this scenario, the deferred interest would be $1,592.00 per month that would be allowed to wrap around to the principal balance of the homebuyer's loan. The reader should now understand why the life cap is a critical aspect that needs to be taken into consideration when considering an adjustable loan program.

Furthermore, again in my professional opinion, lenders should not be allowed to have any interest rate life caps greater than 9.500 percent applied to an adjustable-interest-rate loan program. Lenders should be restricted to using a maximum life cap of 9.500 percent, as this is more than enough in the form of additional interest profits to the lending institutions, regardless of how high interest-rate figures go in the future. Furthermore, a 9.500 percent life cap would still be a reasonable and fair life cap for the home-buying public that is seeking an adjustable-interest-rate loan program.

Dangerous Start Rates to Avoid

For homebuyers, the start rate is just one of the wonderful aspects of the adjustable option loan. The start rate grants homebuyers the ability to make a low monthly mortgage interest payment, while at the same time allowing homebuyers the right to make the monthly mortgage principal-and-interest payment based on the note rate, should they elect to do so, anytime they want during the term of their loan. However, homebuyers must understand that the greater the difference is between the start rate and the note rate, the greater the profit will be to the lenders.

For example, let us assume that prospective homebuyers are being qualified for their home loan by lenders at the note rate of, let's say, 7.500 percent, and yet they are being offered a start rate of, let's say, .500 percent. As enticing as this may be to homebuyers, the lenders are gouging homebuyers in the form of deferred interest while they are laughing all the way to the bank with the homebuyers' monies. Homebuyers need to think about this for a minute. If homebuyers are qualified for their home loan at the note rate and approved, that means that they have the ability to make the monthly mortgage principal-and-interest payments to the lenders. So why would homebuyers even think about accepting a start rate payment based on .500 percent? Sure, the initial monthly mortgage loan payments will be considerably low, but why should homebuyers continue to line the pockets of the lenders in the form of outrageous deferred interest?

In my professional opinion, if homebuyers can qualify for a home loan based on the note rate, then homebuyers should not accept anything less than 3 percent or 4 percent below the note rate as their start rate. By closing the gap between the start rate and the note rate, homebuyers limit the amount of profit that the lenders will be able to make on the option loan. Likewise, homebuyers can also limit the amount of deferred interest that lenders are able to realize simply by closing the gap between the start rate and the note rate.

Let's look at an example. Using a home loan finance figure of $350,000.00 having a start rate of .500 percent, homebuyers would have a monthly mortgage loan payment of $1,047.00. However, homebuyers should be making a monthly mortgage loan payment of $2,447.00 based on the note rate of 7.500 percent. By subtracting the difference, it can be seen that a homebuyer's monthly mortgage loan would be subjected to $1,400.00 in deferred interest that would wrap around to the balance of their home loan. However, should a homebuyer elect to have a start rate payment based on 3.500 percent instead of the .500 percent payment be offered by the lenders, the monthly mortgage loan payment would be $1,572.00, and the homeowner would now be subjected to approximately $875.00 per month in deferred interest payments, thereby cutting the profit to the lenders by $525.00 per month. Simply by choosing a higher start rate, the homebuyer managed to cut $31,500.00 off the mortgage loan in the form of deferred interest payments that would have otherwise gone to the lender over a five-year period of time.

It is, therefore, my professional opinion that lenders should not be allowed to offer start rates that are more than four percentage points below their associated note rates. Furthermore, even at four percentage points below the note rates, the lenders will still make considerable amounts of money on these loan programs. Start rates that are more than four percentage points below their associated note rates basically become a detriment to homebuyers, and in turn make more money for the lenders, thereby increasing the loan yield, which in turn allows the lenders to make even more money on these loans when they sell them in the secondary market, all at the expense of the unsuspecting homebuyers.

Nevertheless, if homebuyers can qualify for a home loan at the note rate, they will be way ahead of the game if they accept a start rate as close to the note rate as possible, preferably within two or three percentage points below the note rate, as this would limit the tremendous profit to the lenders, as well as, giving homebuyers all of the advantages of the option loan that they are entitled to; after all, the banks were the ones who invented this loan program in the first place. Likewise, any start rate being offered by any lender at more than four percentage points below the note rate should be classified as being dangerous or even predatory lending as far as the prospective homebuyers are concerned.

Unfortunately, the majority of people in the lending industry lack the qualifications, knowledge, and education that are required in order to fully understand how these option loan programs work, and how they function, and to explain or even being capable of charting the inner workings of these loan programs to the complete understanding of prospective homebuyers. As stated earlier, approximately 80 percent to 90 percent of all mortgage loans being offered to the unsuspecting home-buying public in California are comprised of these option loan programs, without the slightest explanation as to how the loan programs work. Furthermore, and because of the tremendous amount of profit that the option loans generate, I am now seeing the option loan being used more and more by various lenders throughout the rest of the states in the United States, and again, without any explanations to the unsuspecting homebuyers as to how these option loan programs work.

Ladies and Gentlemen, it doesn't get more dangerous than this, especially, when one understands that buying a home may be the single largest cash outlay and investment that the majority of the general home-buying public will ever make in their lifetime. And to think that these homebuyers are being given a loan program that is not even partially understood, let alone completely understood, by the majority of the mortgage loan consultants, loan officers, and lenders throughout the mortgage loan industry, is a dangerous situation for the homebuyers. The offering of these loan programs by mortgage loan consultants, loan officers, and lenders without qualifications, knowledge, or education is not only a very dangerous and scary proposition, but it also becomes a situation that is extremely detrimental to the general home-buying public. Homebuyers who are being given these option loan programs without having any idea of how these loan programs work are subject to becoming foreclosure statistics in the near future without having the slightest idea of what happened or how it happened to them, because thought they were getting a good home loan, as it was inadequately explained to them by their uneducated and untrained mortgage loan consultant, loan officer or their direct lender.

Homebuyers need to understand that as it currently stands throughout the United States, in order to become a mortgage loan consultant or loan officer, one only needs to pass a real-estate salesperson exam, and then have the financial staying ability needed in order to learn the mortgage loan business, that is usually accomplished by trial and error. Other than the trial-and-error learning process, there is very little, if any, ongoing training available in the mortgage loan business. Unfortunately, this is the reason for the tremendous lack of knowledge and education that is required to become proficient in the mortgage loan business, and why the unsuspecting home buying public is being jeopardized and forced into losing their homes to foreclosures.

Back in the early 1990s, I realized that the training and education of prospective mortgage loan consultants, and loan officers was needed to allow them to become proficient in the mortgage loan business. Therefore, I sat down, and after two years of writing and organizing a training manual, my wife and I opened the Professional Loan Officer Training Center, which was located in Lake Forrest, California. Our course was intensive, and for three hours each day for two weeks we trained anyone who was already in the mortgage loan business or wanted to become a mortgage loan consultant or a bank loan officer. We ended training approximately 75 percent of all of the brokers that were located in the Orange County area of Southern California during that period of time. Moreover, for the next three and one-half years, we maintained standing room only as the word about our training center spread, and our graduates came into major demand by the various banking institutions, and lenders inside and outside of the Orange County area. In order for our trainees to receive a passing grade, they each had to make up a complete loan application package, real or created, along with a loan program recommendation complete with a full explanation as to how the loan program functioned in all aspects.

The Professional Loan Officer Training Center maintained a 97 percent passing grade average, and our mortgage loan consultants and loan officers walked out of our facility having the equivalent of five or more years of knowledge and education behind them when they graduated. For resumes, we simply had the graduates submit their loan application packages to the prospective lenders they wanted to work with, and the training facility maintained a 99 percent hiring factor with our graduates. However, like all good things, the refinancing boom came to an abrupt halt and we ended up training only one person in the following fifteen months, and because we had bills to pay and kids to take care of and feed, we ended up closing the training facility.

As far as I know, there hasn't been another loan officer training facility available anywhere in the United States as educationally intensive as the Professional Loan Officer Training Center was. And as sad as it may be, the need for educated and knowledgeable mortgage loan consultants and loan officers remains, and they are in dire need of advance education throughout the United States. However, for homebuyers that have managed to get their hands on this book, the information contained herein will place you light years ahead of the majority of the mortgage loan consultants, loan officers, and lenders that are currently in the mortgage loan business today. Furthermore, it will give you the education and knowledge you should have in order to make an adequate assessment of any mortgage loan programs mentioned in this book, as well as, those mortgage loan programs that I have not covered, because you will be prepared to ask the appropriate critical questions you need to in order to understand any mortgage loan program on the market today, and any that may arise in the future. Likewise, the personal knowledge one will glean from this book, will allow one to run circles around the majority of bankers if, and when, you decide to purchase a home.

The Reverse Mortgage

The only reason that I am going to elucidate on this subject is because people are always asking me, and wanting to know about the advantages and disadvantages of "The Reverse Mortgage," So, let's get started.

Like most everything else, there are both good and bad aspects of the reverse mortgage. The reverse mortgage was initially established in 1961by Nelson Haynes in Portland, Maine, while he was working for Deering Savings and Loan for a recent widow named Nellie Young who was struggling to make ends meet. Because of Nelson's generosity and kindness towards Nellie, this type of financing revolutionized the mortgage industry. However, in 1987 federal insurance for reverse mortgages was passed by Congress and signed by President Ronald Reagan in 1988. Since then, there have been continued updated advancements, in addition to increases in FHA loan limits for 2018 are currently set at $625,500. Nevertheless, one has to be 62 years old or older, and interested in financing home improvements, or supplement retirement income, or pay for healthcare expenses, or paying off the current mortgage. The nation's consumer protection agency is the "Federal Trade Commission" (FTC), and the FHA is responsible for funding approximately 90 percent of all reverse mortgages under the heading of the "Home Equity Conversion Mortgage" (HECM) in today's marketplace.

Currently there are three kinds of reverse mortgages available in today's marketplace as follows: 1) The single-purpose reverse mortgages, offered by some local state governments and nonprofit organizations that are the least expensive, and can only be used for purposes specified by the government or the nonprofit lenders. Homeowners with low or limited income can usually qualify for this type of loan. For details concerning this loan consult your lender.

2) The "Home Equity Conversion Mortgage" (HECM) is backed by the U.S. Department of Housing and Urban Development (HUD). However, the HECM and proprietary reverse mortgages can be more expensive than regular home financing including the upfront costs and even though this reverse mortgage is readily available, it has no income or medical requirements, and can be used for any reason. However, before applying for the HECM there is also a requirement for the people to meet with a counselor, and you can request that the counselor assist you by comparing the cost of the different reverse mortgages. As of the year 2000, detailed limits concerning origination fees charged by lenders are allowable and were approved by Congress from a minimum of $2,500.00 to a maximum of $6,000.00, which is now the law.

3) The proprietary reverse mortgages are usually backed by companies that develop them, and issue private loans. However, for those who are interested in these reverse mortgage loans, there is a myriad of information available on the internet, as well as, the FHA, HUD and other organizations.

Moreover, home owners can choose different payment options such as: Fixed monthly cash advances for a specified period of time called a "Term Option." There is also a fixed monthly cash withdrawal as long as you live in your home called a "Tenure Option." There is a line of credit that allows you to withdraw the loan monies at any time, and in any amounts you want until the line of credit proceeds have been used up. Likewise, you can have a line of credit along with monthly payments, and the homeowner can change their payment options any time they want for a fee that will be plus or minus $20.00 or so to make the change. As a rule these loans have to be paid back when people sell their homes, or when the surviving borrower dies, or when one no longer uses their home as their principal resident. An owner can also live in a nursing home or medical facility for a year before they have to repay the loan. Furthermore, people with reverse mortgages must continue to pay their property taxes and insurance, as well as, the up keep on their properties even though there is no tax charged for the use of the reverse mortgage monies. The people should also know that the loan interest on a reverse mortgage will continue to accrue on the loan balance every year, thereby increasing the loan balance should the people elect not to pay down the reverse mortgage balance. Likewise, for those of you who decide to get an HECM reverse mortgage, you will be required to pay a 1.25 percent insurance premium each year on the remaining loan balance because the loan is being insured by the FHA.

As for the bad aspects of the reverse mortgage, and in our opinion, and even though this loan was originally designed to assist elderly persons who are having trouble, and struggling to make ends meet, the reverse mortgage today, like the reverse mortgages in the years gone by, is designed to let the lenders steal your home along with the rest of your home equity. Question: Why does our government always start advertising, and promoting the reverse mortgage when interest rates are at their lowest point? Answer: Because this is when the government, and private lenders can make the most money when they take your home back in order to pay back the loan, and then they steal the rest of the equity that is left in the home.

I am not going to go into the various calculations that will be required to determine the amount of equity people will be able to withdraw from their homes for a reverse mortgage, as the lenders will make these calculations if and when people decide to get a reverse mortgage. Currently, people can withdraw around 60 percent of their total home equity, but this percentage will be changing in a short period of time, so check with your reverse mortgage lender. In addition, people with very little mortgage balances left on their homes can also include these balances to pay off their homes when they apply for a reverse mortgage loan. Likewise, there will be new limits on the amount of monies that people can take out in their first year of the reverse mortgage that will probably hurt the most needy and poor potential borrowers. What this all boils down to is people will only be able to get approximately 60 percent of the appraised value of their home as indicated by FHA, less fees.

Basically, this is all designed by the Reverse Mortgage Lenders Association who think and believe that these changes might influence the people to apply for what they need and no more. First of all, who do these association people think they are? Just how do these pranksters figure that the people will know exactly what they will need in the way of reverse mortgage monies? According to the association, people apply for what they need, and no more, is an absolute joke! First of all, these homes belong to the people, and not even the people know how long they will live in their homes, let alone how much money they will need, and for how long they will need the money. Furthermore, to have some association attempt to tell the people to take only what they need, tells us, that these association personnel are either smoking something or taking something that is distorting their thought processes. Secondly, all that this is going to accomplish, is that it will make it harder to get access to a reverse mortgage, which in turn, will eventually, cause another reverse mortgage loan program to emerge into the reverse mortgage loan marketplace, as there is just too much money to be made by the lenders for them to leave it on the table.

Anyways, let's get back on subject as to the bad aspects of the reverse home mortgage. In the event that a homeowner does not have anyone to leave their home to in the way of family, relatives, friends, or in the way of a donation, then a reverse mortgage may be a good way to go to live out the rest of their lives with extra monies. However, if one wants to leave their property to their loved one's and at the same time they get a reverse mortgage, the chances are, they will lose their home to the federal or state government, or a private reverse mortgage lender. Why? Simple! All of these lenders are aware of the national statistics concerning household incomes, and the saving habits of the people, and they know that the odds are in their favor. Example: Let's do a very simple calculation, and say that your home is appraised at $200,000.00, and you can get a reverse mortgage for 60 percent of the appraised value for 10, 20 or 25 years. We now take the $200,000.00, and multiply this figure by 60 percent, and you get a figure of $120,000.00. Now, take the 120,000.00 figure, and divide it by 10 years, and you get an annual figure of $12,000.00 that you again divide by 12, that represents the 12 months of the year, and you get a figure of $1,000.00. This would technically be the monthly income that you would be entitled to receive with a reverse mortgage for ten years. Likewise, if you wanted to have these monies distributed for 20 years, you would be entitled to $6,000.00 per year, or $500.00 per month, and for 25 years, you would receive $4,800.00 per year, or $400.00 per month. Remember, this is a very simple calculation to give the reader an idea of what you can expect in monthly income from a reverse mortgage. Furthermore, the real calculations for a reverse mortgage will be determined by the lender you choose to do business with, and remember, everything is negotiable in any real estate transaction.

Okay, based on the above scenario, and assuming your loved one passes in ten years, whoever the home is left to will now have to come up with $120,000.00 to pay back the reverse mortgage loan plus the interest at, and let's say 5 percent on the monies for 10 years, which is an additional $60,000.00 in order to keep the home in the family, that now becomes approximately $180,000.00 the family will need in order to payback the lender to retain the home. Moreover, and assuming the home appreciated, and we are not in a depressed housing market, your loved ones home should now be worth about $250,000.00, and after paying off the $180,000.00 you would still have approximately $70,000.00 equity left in the home that was bequeathed to you from your loved one. However, the only problem with this scenario is that all the reverse mortgage lenders know that the chances of people coming up with this kind of money is this side of impossible, and the lenders will end up with your loved one's home. The reverse mortgage lenders know that only 1 to 3 percent of these entire inherited properties will ever be paid off by the families even if these families have a year or more to sell the home they inherited. These families will also have the opportunity to borrow the money, or take out a second, assuming they own a home and can qualify, or more than likely they will let the home be taken back by the reverse mortgage lender. Furthermore, when the lenders take the home back, they write off the principal and interest that was owed on the loan, and they now have a property with a minimum equity of $250,000.00 that they will make on this reverse mortgage property. In other words, no matter what the value of the property is, the reverse mortgage loan is another pure rip-off scam devised by the government, in order to continue to make trillions and trillions of dollars off the elderly American homeowner's real estate holdings.

Nevertheless, when the last reverse mortgagor passes, the loan servicers will send a letter indicating the balance of the loan that is due, and an heir or the estate administrator will have 30 days to indicate that the home will be paid or the home sold. However, if no decision is initiated or indicated, then the reverse mortgage lender can start the foreclosure process. Likewise, I suggest that the people consider other alternatives to a reverse mortgage such as selling your home and downsizing your living accommodations. Furthermore, and if you can afford the payments, people would be better off considering a cash out refinance that would also cost them less money than a reverse mortgage. Moreover, should people be approaching retirement, or are in retirement, they may want to consider buying another book that was released in January of 2015, entitled "HOW ANYONE CAN RETIRE LIVING LARGE ON PENNIES." This book can be purchased at Amazon.com, Createspace.com, or Kindle. This book reveals several saving techniques relating to cash monies, social security monies, downsizing, reinvesting and saving monies every month, and how to put these monies back into one's retirement accounts, just to mention a few topics, as this book is filled with many savings techniques. This retirement book will also show people how to live below their means, and at the same time, show them how they can become well-off and well-to-do before they reach retirement or if they are already in retirement, and never having to worry about going back to work again in order to survive in their retirement years. In our opinion, and as mentioned early on, unless one does not want to leave their home to family members, relatives, friends, or in the way of a donation, then a reverse mortgage may be a good way to go to live out the rest of their lives having extra monies, and no more home mortgage loan payments. On the other hand, should people considering a reverse mortgage, and have family, relatives, friends, or they intend to make a donation of their home, then people should, at all costs, stay away from a reverse mortgage unless the people know that their family, relatives, or friends, have the financial capability to pay back the reverse mortgage loan including interest.

The Intelligent Smart Way to Buy a Home without Going Broke or ever Losing your Home

We are now going to show you why you cannot get ahead, and talk about your monthly income for a minute. In the old days one's income was divided into 4 representing the 4 weeks in a month where 25% of one's monthly income went towards the house payment, 25% went towards the bills, 25% went towards running the household, and the last 25% of the monthly income was put away for savings. During these times people had plenty of time to save money, go on vacations, and just have a good old time until the government, specifically, the Democrats, decided that the people had too much freedom to roam around the country and do whatever they wanted whenever they wanted to, making it difficult for the government to keep track of the people. However, as time has gone by, things started becoming more and more expensive, and one's monthly income had to be restructured by the government and the banks to reflect a 3rd of one's income, which now needed to be divided into the 4 weeks of the month in order to get by, and notice we did not say get ahead. Where a 3rd of one's income went towards the house payment and another 3rd went towards the bills, and the final 3rd of one's income was supposed to cover the cost of running the household, and if anything was left over, it was to go towards savings. Unfortunately, this new development of using a 1/3rd, 1/3rd, and 1/3rd of one's monthly income caused people to lose the majority of their discretionary spending income. This in turn had major repercussions on the government and the infrastructure because it forced the people to curtail their spending in the retail markets thereby causing a major slowdown in our economy throughout the United States.

Let's now view the reason why millions and millions of people lose their homes when the economy goes into a financial recession, economic recession, or when the housing market goes upside down, causing their home values to become less than what the homeowners originally paid for their home.

Years ago, housing ratios were established at 28/36 percent where the 28 percent figure was to be allocated towards the monthly mortgage payment for principal and interest (PI), and the 36 percent figure was designed to allow people to enjoy a reasonable standard of family living by carrying some debt. However, these ratios will fluctuate depending on the financial institutional guidelines of the mortgage lender the homebuyers decide to use to finance their home.

Nevertheless, it is what the government and banks didn't tell you that would make it almost impossible for you to get ahead, let alone save any money for your future in the event you purchased a home. Even to this day, homeownership is touted by the government and banks as being the ultimate American Dream even though you can easily lose your home, and your entire equity in the blink of an eye. What the government and banks don't tell you is that you cannot afford to buy a home based on your gross monthly income.

In today's housing market, and according to Zillow, the average home sales price today across the United States is $215,600.00. However, how long this average sales price remains in the housing market will be determined on how the economy fluctuates now and in the future. In order to give you an example of the intelligent and smart way to buy a home, and not have to worry about losing your home unless, of course, there is no more household income to pay the mortgage, we are going to look at the three scenarios.

Example A -- Let's say that you want to buy a home for $200,000.00, and you want a mortgage payment of $1,200.00 a month to cover the total PITI. Since we are currently in a 4.5 percent to 5.5 percent interest rate market, I will use my formula based on a multiple of 4 at the 5 percent interest rate figure, which means you need a gross monthly income of $4,800.00 to qualify for, and buy a home at $200,000.00 with a 20 percent down payment of $40.000.00 according to the government and the banks, and end up within the guidelines of having excellent ratios, including adding approximately $456.00 in outgoing debt. Technically speaking, the homebuyer will end up with a ratio of 27/36, and since the established ratios are 28/36 you would be able to buy this $200,000.00 home in this low interest rate market. However, the homebuyer must remember that any amount of outgoing debts will increase their monthly mortgage payment. Looking at the above scenario, and by including the $456.00 in outgoing debt, this increases the homebuyers' outgoing mortgage payment to $1,728.00 each and every month. So, be careful of how much outgoing debt you are willing to carry, especially, if the buyers only want a $1,200.00 (plus or minus) in a monthly mortgage payment. Nevertheless, in the above calculations the homebuyers will be buying a $200,000.00 home, having a $40,000.00 down payment, and financing $160,000.00 at 5 percent interest for 30 years. The principal and interest payment for this mortgage loan will be $859.00, the taxes will be $333.00, and the home insurance will be $80.00 for a total of $1272.00 in PITI, which is only $72.00 more than the buyers requested for their monthly mortgage loan payment. Nevertheless, the homebuyers do not have the slightest idea that they cannot afford this home even though they are qualified to purchase this home according to the government and banks. We are now going to show you why millions of people continue to lose their homes in a high interest rate market, or the economy goes into a recession, financial recession, or when the housing market goes upside down.

We are going to use the same figure of $200,000.00 for the home purchase price having the same down payment, the 5 percent interest rate, and the same $1,200.00 monthly mortgage payment, with the same monthly income of $4800.00 the buyers think they can afford, only this time we are going to use the buyers' *"Net Income"* or the actual real monthly income after deducting for income taxes. Assuming a tax bracket of approximately 25 percent, we end up deducting $1,200.00 from the gross monthly income of $4,800.00 the government and banks use, and we now have an income of $3,600.00 of actual real monthly dollars that the buyers can afford to spend on a home after taxes. Okay, based on the above net income figures the homebuyers can afford to purchase a home for $144,000.00 minimum or a maximum of $160,000.00 and technically never have to worry or concern themselves about losing their home.

Example B -- With the buyer's real net income and a home sales price of $144,000.00, the buyers only need a down payment of $28,800.00 financing $115,200.00 for 30 years at 5 percent interest. This would make the monthly PITI payment $882.00 giving the buyers a 25 percent front-end ratio, and allowing them to carry debt of $414.00 making the back-end 36 percent or 25/36. Analyzing the money difference between the $200,000.00 home using the buyers' gross income, and the $144,000.00 home using the buyers' net income, the buyers would save $11,200.00 just in the down payment. The buyers would also save $390.00 a month in the PITI mortgage payments for a savings of $4,692.00 each year. Nevertheless, and depending on the amount of the buyers outgoing payments, the savings could be less.

Example C -- On the other hand, the buyers could elect to purchase a home for $160,000.00 having a down payment of $32,000.00, financing $128,000.00 for 30 years at 5 percent interest. In this situation the buyers would have a monthly PITI payment of $1,007.00 with a front ratio of 28 percent, and carrying a debt of $289.00 giving them a back-end ratio of 36 percent or 28/36, which would be the lenders standard maximum ratios. In this scenario the buyers would save $8,000.00 in the way of a down payment vs. Example A, and $265.00 in monthly PITI payments or $3,180.00 per year, and again, depending on the outgoing home payments.

Looking at **Example A**, the chances of these people surviving in a high interest rate market, a recession, or when the housing market goes upside down will be slim to none. Why? Because these people are basically living from paycheck to paycheck because of using their gross income to qualify for a higher home value when their real net income in **Examples B and C** is their only usable income as the gross income is a fantasy, because these monies do not belong to them. Furthermore, in **Example A**, the buyers probably have not taken into consideration the additional payments for *Food* (that can be a major household expense), not to mention *Gas, Electric, Trash, Phone, Internet, Car or Truck payments and expenses, Household and Property Maintenance, and*

Property Taxes, if the homebuyers did not elect to impound their property taxes. And don't forget possible **Association fees**, if you bought in an association, and don't forget your **Medical Insurance fees.**

Therefore, and contrary to what the government and banks are trying to get away with when it comes to the American Dream of owning a home, using your gross monthly income to qualify for a home that you cannot afford is an atrocity, that comes under the heading of *MALUM IN SE in Latin,* that means*, evil in itself or naturally evil as adjudged by a civilized society*, which in my opinion, is what explains our government and the banking lending system in the United States housing market known as greed. Likewise, when we now look back at **Examples A and C**, and compare the ratios based on the buyers real net income, their real ratios now become 35/48, which indicates that the buyers cannot afford a $200,000.00 home even though the government and the banks inform the buyers that they are qualified to make the purchase. Moreover, if you are planning to purchase a home, and are tempted to use your gross monthly income in order to qualify for more of a home than you can afford, and end up using the government and banks ratios of 28/36 percent, just remember, you are playing with fire. When someone tells you that your real housing ratios are 35/48 percent, using your real net monthly income after taxes, that should tell you that you are now living from paycheck to paycheck, and the slightest drop in the economy, you could end up in foreclosure and out in the street so fast that you won't have time to blink, so use your head. Furthermore, and the only way to avoid this situation is to put down as a down payment of at least 50 percent of the home value, and you will never have to worry about losing your home no matter what the government, banks or the economy does now or in the future.

Think about this for a moment, if your home is paid off, or you have a very low mortgage loan balance, what do you have? You have your own bank, you have an unlimited source of money if and when you need it, or an income for the rest of your life if you choose to do a Reverse Mortgage providing you do not have anyone left in the family to pass something onto in the form of an inheritance. Once your home is paid off, or has a very low mortgage loan balance, you no longer have a liability to worry about, as your home has turned into an asset providing you keep the property taxes and insurance paid, and up to date. And the best part about this scenario is that no one can take your property away from you or force foreclosure proceedings, unless of course, you get yourself into a situation that allows this process to take place.

Another avenue people may want to consider when buying a home is to consider using FHA financing, as they only require a 3.5 percent down payment, however, the people need to understand what they may be getting themselves into as FHA will go as high as financing $679,650.00 in *"High Cost"* areas such as New York, Washington D. C., Los Angeles and San Francisco, and other areas of the country. For *"Low Cost"* areas the loan limits will be $292,515.00, but the people will have to call the FHA or an FHA lender to get a list of these areas. Also, the current conforming loan limits remain at $453,100.00, and the FHA's loan limit floor is stilled figured as 65percent of these loans, which will usually remain in effect for one year, so be sure to check with a lender every year starting in January of every New Year. Nevertheless, just remember to use your net income as opposed to your gross income when buying a home, whether the lender is a conventional lender or an FHA lender, so you can pretty much guarantee yourselves of not losing your home should the United States goes into a high interest rate market, or the economy goes into a recession, or the housing market goes upside down again now or anytime in the future.

Likewise, and before we end this part of the book, we would just like to point out to the people, that by using ones net income to purchase a home, you may not get the home you want and desire this time. However, knowing that you will not lose your home, no matter what happens is a very comforting feeling or thought. Furthermore, and as in Joan's and my situation, we lived in a very well to do area in Laguna Niguel, California after we got married, but because we realized that we were being balled and chained financially to Joan's condominium, we ended up downsizing to a mobile home from the condo. By doing so, we nevertheless ended up downgrading and living below our means for several years in order to save our income, and be able to eventually up grade far and beyond our previous living standards. By taking a back seat, so to speak, today we live in a beautiful home in a very well to do upper class neighborhood knowing full well that we will never have to work again in our lifetimes. By doing the things that we have explained to the readers in this book, we are now able to do anything we want, anytime we want, and buying what we want anytime we desire something. Likewise, our favorite thing to do is eating out every day of the week, and we will continue to do so as long as we can in our retirement years. We also get to meet and converse with all kinds of people having very diversified backgrounds, and we love it, and we wish the same things for you. Remember, anything is possible when one puts their mind to it, and never give up trying no matter how many times one gets knocked down, just get back up and try again, again, and again until you reach the objectives you want to achieve. One last piece of advice, Never be in a hurry to buy a home as you will pay too much, and never sell in a hurry as you will lose a considerable amount of money on your transaction. Should anyone desire to know how to negotiate on anything, you can purchase my other book entitled "How Anyone Can Retire Living Large on Pennies."

GO FOR IT, AND BEST WISHES!
WISHING YOU INTELLIGENT AND SMART
HOME BUYING ADVENTURES.

BONUS SECTION

Preface

I have been a Loan Officer in the real estate business for many years and you get to meet all sorts of people. One such encounter happened back in the 80's when by accident I walked through a bank loan officer's door without knocking. When the door opened, here was this guy throwing wiffle ball darts at a dart board that was covered in velcro, and depending on where the wiffle dart landed he would take the file in front of him and either put it on the right or left side of his desk. When this guy turned around, you could tell by his facial expression that I was not the one who he had been expecting. This bank loan officer, (we will call Joe) turned out to be the bank's Branch Manager of a major California Bank and its Commercial Lending Officer. Nevertheless, I introduced myself and told Joe that I was interested in learning the in's and out's of the bank's real estate loan division, and how they determine who they will accept and who they will not accept as loan prospects that were interested in buying a home.

To make a long story short, Joe and I became very close friends over the years, and when I asked him what he was doing with the wiffle darts, he said he was the bank's Loan Committee who determined who would and who would not be granted a real estate loan from his particular bank. According to Joe, he had a wiffle ball dart system and depending on where the wiffle dart landed on the wiffle target, the people's home loan files were either stamped approved or denied. So, the real estate application files were then placed on the right of Joe's desk for funding or on the left side of his desk for the turndown real estate loans, and that is how Joe ran this bank when it came to real estate loans.

Joe had spent fifteen years in the banking business and was a member of The American Institute of Banking. This is a great organization that functions as the educational arm of banking. A large part of banking education is bankers teaching other bankers. This is greatly needed as the banking industry is constantly changing everyday. More importantly, is the fact that this knowledge has been omitted from teaching the basic concepts of credit and banking to the American people.

Throughout this writing, I will offer some of Joe's helpful suggestions and scenarios we talked about, along with my real estate banking experience input that will assist the reader to become familiar, and, to get a better understanding of banking credit. Both Joe and I have noticed that most bank customers do not know the people in the banks or how to use the banks to their advantage. Our hope is that this writing will assist you in establishing and expanding your credit needs with a better understanding of what bankers are looking for in basic credit.

People in Banking

For years, the banking profession has been held in esteem in regard to integrity, honesty, and intelligence. When one looks at the people in their community, one will generally find a banker. However, in the past three or four decades the respectability has given way to negative publicity that some banks and bankers have given to the profession. Most of this negative publicity occurred during the financial meltdown in the early part of the year 2007 and is still causing problems all because of the greed by the banking institutions. Nevertheless, the banking industry will continue to feel the ripple effects of this bad publicity for some time to come in the future.

In today's modern society one has to realize that a banker does not have the ability to be a total banker as it is an impossibility. In today's society the banking industry is far more sophisticated and complex than it has been in years past. With the proliferation of the computers there has been a development of several new positions that have opened up in the banks. Likewise, banking is world wide and requires knowledge concerning international finance, money transfer, etc. Along with this, major banks have trust departments offering several specialized services that requires numerous positions of various skills. Therefore, since we are in an age of specialization, banks can no longer afford to be total bankers.

Usually, people progressed through a career in banking starting in the bookkeeping department for a few years, then worked their way up into the lending and management areas. This was acceptable until the 1960s when the industry began expanding at a very rapid rate. Bankers then started looking around and found that there were very few qualified people coming into the banking profession and there wasn't sufficient time to train these new people. Some of the major banks started formal management programs to advance the new employees to fill these new positions. This is where one of the major banking dilemmas started. A new employee would be trained and then placed into a position after two years under someone who took 25 years to attain that same position. We have heard often, how long term employees would grumble and complain, "it took me 20 years to reach that salary level and I will not recommend him." At that time the industry had a lot of this thinking going on in the late 50's and 60's.

It should also be pointed out, even in specialized fields, that it could take several years of maturity to achieve total knowledge in one's area of expertise. Now that we have moved into the 21st Century, we find an industry that is replete with three types of employees: the bright young person who is eager to learn but does not have the time or experience needed to be successful. Next, we have the individual who for some unknown reason has been elevated to a position which is beyond their maximum potential. Lastly, we have that person who is very good and becomes a competent banker.

Here I would like to acquaint you with whom you are usually going to be dealing with when you walk into the majority of banks in America. According to my friend Joe he indicates and admits that the aforementioned stated above will cover the majority of people in the banking business even today. Joe had worked as a banker for over 15 years, and according to him, there was only one person in the Midwest who could be called a total banker. It is also interesting to note that this person did not go to college and had no degrees. Nevertheless, we have all met this type of individual that excels at anything they set out to do.

As we stated previously, it is important to get to know your banker. Likewise, you should get to know the proper people in your bank. What we have observed over the years is that the majority of bank customers only get to know the tellers. However, it is imperative that you get to know the president or vice president and the bank manager in your bank. Even if you have to go out of your way and take some extra time to do so. The goal here is to make a positive introduction and don't introduce yourself with a complaint like why did the bank not honor my check?

The next thing you want to do is to analyze the type and size of the banking system. If you reside in a state that has branch banking, be sure to get to know the branch manager and/or the assistant branch manager. If you decide to open an account, ask to be introduced to the managers and don't be embarrassed about the size of the account you are opening as this is the best time to be meeting the manager. Likewise, the manager will not know the size of your account and if he/she finds out later that your account is a small account, he/she will view your potential rather than the actual amount that you invested in the bank at that time. Nonetheless, if you think or feel that you are not meeting the right person, then we suggest that there are other banks you can go to that have and offer the same services. Remember, banking is a business and if you are not satisfied, don't hesitate to change banks.

Now, once you think or feel that you have met the proper person, be sure to say something positive. If you are young and new to the world of banking, ask the manager if you can stop by for some advice every now and then. If you are in college, tell them you are doing a paper and would appreciate getting their thoughts on a given subject. Furthermore, if you are already established in a profession or working situation, ask for some future advice that is related to what you are doing. By doing these simple things, you are meeting the right people and establishing follow-up conversations. Moreover, you are placing yourself in the bankers mind. Be sure when you come into the bank that you wave at these people and if they are not busy, stop by for a friendly hello. However, don't make a nuisance of yourself, but let them know that you are their customer.

Should your bank be one of the many smaller independent banks throughout America, you should do exactly the same thing. After you have opened your account or accounts, get to know one of the loan officers and stop by to say hello and follow the same procedures you would have in a branch bank. Here, too, you could make an appointment to meet one of the senior officers for an interview concerning your paper. Likewise, for the established worker or business man/woman you, too, can meet the same banking personnel, but don't hesitate to ask questions related to your business or profession and how it fits into the current economy. Ask the banker for his/her opinion on the economy and how it's trending. Remember, bankers are people, too, and they like to feel that they are on top of the current economic events and they will be honored to give you some excellent advice.

On the other hand, if you are doing business with one of the larger banks in America that has no branches, then most of their loan officers will be located on other floors and in other departments in the bank. The nice thing about these banks is that they have personal banking officers who are able to help you with your beginning banking needs. However, most of them will have limited credit authority but they can assist you with establishing your initial credit up to a certain amount. Again, we can't stress enough on the importance of getting to know your banker, be it the president, vice president or managers. This process is not something that will happen overnight, but it takes time, maybe a couple of years to develop a good relationship with the bank personnel, but it will be well worth it in the long run.

Learning to Use Your Bank

Over the years Joe and I found out that the majority of people do not know how to use the banks in America to establish their credit and fulfill their credit needs and requirements. We have noticed that the majority of people do not understand how banks work and how to go about establishing themselves with credit at an early age so that when they get older they will have all the credit they will need.

It was also interesting for us to note that a number of successful people in their chosen field did not understand the basic concepts of borrowing money or the extent of their financial capabilities. To some extent, the information and examples cited herein by Joe may seem common place, but to others the process of borrowing money and establishing credit has created a great deal of frustration and turmoil and has been a source of great concern in the banking industry. One common situation that Joe and I have encountered over and over again is the solid young customer who is being turned down on a credit request because they were too new on their job or they did not have an established past credit background. We will try to show you how you can acquire a credit background so that by the time a person is in their early twenties they will have established banking credit. We also know that having a proven past banking credit background is a very positive fact on anyone's credit report.

The educational system in America is good at teaching theory, but a practical application of facts on banking and how they work is never offered. We both feel especially strong on this point when it comes to the medical profession. Here is a very skilled group of people who have a high degree of intelligence, but have a difficult time managing their own monies. It would be extremely worth while if the colleges would offer a course on basic banking practices for all professions and especially the medical profession. It would also be helpful if the high schools would offer a course on basic banking practices, specifically, on how to balance checkbooks and what to look for in reconciliation of a bank checking account.

We want to give the reader some insight that will make you more aware of what goes on in a bank and how it can benefit you. The following points will be important by indicating the things that will be needed for you to establish a good financial beginning at the bank of your choice. Over the years we have we seen several interesting situations develop with customers.

We also know from our observance of people and their financial needs that approximately 90% of all the people do not understand how credit works and how they can establish themselves so they will have a proper credit background in order to help them expand their own personal financial goals. We would also like to point out some of Joe's actual cases of customers he has worked with over the years. Each of these cases will point out how most people do not understand how money works and where to acquire it at the lowest cost.

Several years ago Joe told me he was approached by a couple in their mid 50's in a Midwestern bank. These people were part of a growing and expanding computer firm and both of them worked in the math department. During this time they lived in a nice suburban home and were able to sell their home for $26,000.00 of which they only owed $6,000.00. The couple had a gross income of $30,000.00 a year. They had just found their dream home in another suburban community and were about to enter into a real estate sales agreement to purchase this home for 38,000.00. This was a very dramatic experience for this couple, and they were requesting a new 1st mortgage on the property of $18,000.00, and were concerned as to whether they would qualify for the loan. In today's housing market we would assume the above would sound even to the least knowledgeable on credit as quite a solid situation, but we must realize the time was in the late 60's before everything went crazy in the real estate market.

Joe asked the couple to fill out a financial statement and it showed that the couple owned over $180,000.00 of stock in their company. Because the company was growing so fast and was only able to pay stock dividends after it had split five times, they did not realize that they had such a large amount of equity in their company. Needless to say, the couple received their loan and when they found out they had excess income, two years later they paid the $18,000.00 1st mortgage loan off in full. What was interesting here is we have two very talented people having PH D's in mathematics and computer mathematical probability solving for their company, but they were totally unaware of their own personal financial capabilities and how to use it to their advantage.

In another situation that Joe and I discussed was a bank customer who had approach Joe for a small commercial loan to help him expand his business. This customer was forty-six years old and had recently gone through a divorce that turned out to be a true 50-50 split, where he received fifty percent of the liabilities and she received fifty percent of the assets. Nevertheless, in the divorce there was one liability he failed to pay that was a hundred and fifty dollars charge account at a major department store. When he found out about the bill a year and a half later he paid the bill off, but the girl at the counter told him that his credit was ruined forever. Years later this guy remarried and purchased a home for cash and never requested any credit and always paid everything in cash. When this person approached the bank Joe realized that it took this guy a lot of courage to come into a bank to see a loan officer. As this guy was making his loan request, everything was done in a very professional manner for the first part of his request. However, he then began to tell Joe about the hundred and fifty dollars that was a past due charge account at a major department store, which he paid off when he found out about the charge. The funny thing about this situation was that by the time Joe was about finished with the loan papers this guy was ready to turn himself down for the loan. It is interesting to note just how many people do not have a positive attitude and are ready to turn themselves down on their own loan request. Nevertheless, Joe told this guy to stop talking and let him do the talking and explained to him the necessary information the bank would need in order to make a credit decision, and to let Joe advise him about his past credit and how it would affect the credit decision.

It was interesting to note that after checking this guy's credit report background the paid off hundred and fifty dollar charge off never showed up on his credit report. Since then he had maintained a thousand dollar average balance at the bank (later we will explain how this can work to your advantage) and had paid all his fixed payments on time. Also, you may not realize it but even without credit you still have some fixed payments of utilities, property taxes, etc. This guy's new wife had been employed for five years at the same position and his three-year- old company had shown excellent growth. This person was granted his loan for his business and it enabled him to expand adding four more employees. The loan was structured for a three-year loan payoff that was paid off in six months. The forgoing may have sounded like a large credit request, but it was for only a $5,000.00 loan. In this situation here was a good honest person who had one small misgiving about his past and for over seven plus years he felt he was unworthy of credit. The nice thing about this was he sold his mobile home for $45,000.00, and used it for a down payment on a large home, and we were able to give him a mortgage loan commitment for his new home.

We have one more example to relate to the reader and it is about a person who was not a customer at Joe's bank at the time. Joe's bank was approached by a loan company to purchase some of the trust deed loans that it held. At random Joe pulled out one of them and once again we noticed an example that reconfirmed our belief that most people do not understand credit and how or where to acquire it. Here was a person wanting a second mortgage on his personal residence having a first mortgage of $62,000.00 and was requesting a $25,000.00 second mortgage. The home had appraised for $230,000.00 and according to this person's tax returns. he had an adjusted gross income of over $120,000.00 for the last four years. He had been banking at one of the major banks in America and maintained a nice savings account there. At the loan company they had arranged a loan for him at the prime rate plus seven percent at a cost of a 10 point charge. At the time of this person's approval he received the $25,000.00 loan at twenty-one percent for three years at a cost of $2,500.00 in points and his net proceeds were less than $22,500.00. The interesting point here is that this guy's bank was making the same type of loan at 15.5 percent over twenty years at a cost of only 1 point or $250.00 in loan fees.

Many potential customers would qualify at a bank, but they never think of ever asking their own bank. This is a case of an individual who went to the bank every week to deposit his check and never took the additional, time to ask a loan officer if they made second mortgage loans. In this situation the extra time would have saved this person $2,250.00 in loan fees and a lot of interest. There are a few people that you should know on a first name basis: your doctor, dentist, druggist, banker, and service station owner or operator. Over the years we have had several people stop by once a week or so to just say hello. After a while you get to know this person and when credit gets tight or a situation develops, we can guarantee you it's a lot easier to get a loan. Again, the point being made is get to know your banker.

Standard Banking Operations

There are a few basic operational procedures everyone should understand even though there has been several books and manuals written on the subject. There are also some very important things one needs to do to help yourself establish your credit and personal financial future. Some of what we will be saying you may already know, but you should realize the importance of everything. Remember when we were talking about your checking account? When it is handled the right way, it can become a good tool to help you obtain the credit you want or need.

Here are some things most customers don't know: It is important that you know the cut off time at your bank or branch for that day's credit to be applied to your account. Several banks are open until 5 p.m., but their cut off time is 3 p.m. What this means is, if you make a deposit or cash a check before 3 p.m., it will show up on your balance that day. On the other hand, if a transaction is made after 3 p.m., it will not be posted to your account until the next banking business day because the bank computers will consider the transaction to have been made the following day.

For clarification let's view a very common situation where the husband is receiving his paycheck on Friday and he will deposit it at the bank before he comes home. The wife goes out and does her shopping knowing that today is payday. Now, most businesses know that if they deposit before 3 p.m., they will get an extra day's credit in their checking accounts so the store where the wife purchased her morning groceries makes a deposit at 2 p.m. The husband stops by the bank to make his deposit at 5 p.m. on his way home. Both the husband and wife feel that since everything was done the same day that there will be no problem. Technically, the husband and wife are right, but in the real world of banking they are a day late. What happens is that the next day the bank computer prints out an overdraft and their overdraft is recorded in the computer. Hopefully, this will be the husband and wife's first overdraft and they have been customers a long time, in which case the bank will try and call them. In the event contact is not made, their check(s) will probably be returned with a service charge.

There are two points we want to make here. The first is, if you never write a check before you make a deposit you will never be in trouble. The second one is, if you do write a check(s) and you are at the bank to make your deposit, be sure to tell the teller to mark the journal showing your deposit. Doing this will not insure your protection, as new journals come out the next day, but this procedure should help prevent most same-day problems. This is why it is important to remember to balance your bank statements. Learning how to do this in the correct way will assist you in the event you might have any question concerning your account. You can also go to your bank and they will be more than happy to assist you with the proper format. In addition, there are other very important things to remember concerning your monthly statements. Your monthly statement will show a final date of the monthly activity on your account and at the same time showing you the balance in your account as of that date. When you are balancing your account that is the date you work with in your checkbook. Let's say the date of the statement is June 30, but you received your statement on July 11, look at your checkbook register and balance it as of June 30. You will be concerning yourself with checks and deposits made on June 30 or prior. The checks after June 30 will be in your following month's statements. If everything is okay you should have a higher bank statement balance than in your checkbook and that is due to the float factor between your writing checks and when they reach your bank to be paid.

The majority of people do not take the time each month to balance their checkbooks and check to see if they have made a subtraction or an addition error. Because of the float factor you may not show an overdraft, but in the long run it will catch up with you. Therefore, it is vitally important that you balance your checkbook with the bank statement every month. Another crucial situation that is overlooked is to write down each check or debt card purchase in your checkbook register when you write a check and keep an accurate running balance. This may sound like common sense, but it is one of the major areas where people get themselves into trouble.

It may be embarrassing for you while you are at the grocery store to record the check you have just written and subtract out the balance right there at the counter, because there is a big line behind you, and you say that you will remember to do this when you get home. If you only knew how many times people have come to the bank all upset because they received an overdraft notice because they forgot to include the check for $79.95 at the grocery store in their register. They generally come into the bank with the attitude that the bank is wrong. However, after gathering the customer's checks, we ask them how they balanced their last statement and they usually respond by saying it was correct. Next, we ask to see their checkbook register and we usually see that there is no running balance and there are lines running all over the place. It may take several minutes, but we are able to see where most of the checks have a place and then to your customer's amazement, there is the check for $79.95 that's not in their checkbook, which told the computer that the account is overdrawn. By this time the customer who stormed into the bank in total anger and frustration is now very meek and feeling rather foolish.

The situation we really like is where the one spouse comes storming into the bank saying that the bank has made a mistake on their husband's or wife's account. In the majority of situations like this it eventually relates back to one of them not recording a check. Joe related to me where he remembers a man who came storming up to his desk using very bad language. After Joe had gone through this guy's checks, Joe found one check that was not recorded in the register for $300.00 and marked for a new dress for his wife. He then apologized and went out looking for his wife. Needless to say we never did learn what happened after that, but it is fair to assume that he had some serious conversation with his wife that night. The main point we are making here is to record your checks, otherwise an overdraft will be recorded in the computer and will not help you in your request for credit independence.

Furthermore, we do not want to sound like the great defenders of the banking system, but in the case of overdrafts the bank is correct 99% in all situations. So, in the event you have an unpleasant experience of receiving an overdraft notice, realize before you run to the bank that the odds are against you and check your records thoroughly. On the other hand, if you still do not find or see where an error was made, approach the bank in a calm way and you will be surprised with a more positive response.

What's important to remember is that the bank's computer can only read the numbers on the bottom of the check. After you receive your bank statement, you will see in the lower-right hand corner of the check is encoded the amount of the check you have written. This is the amount that the computer will charge your account. It is here that banks will make the largest percentage of mistakes. Let's say you wrote a check for $150.00, but in the lower right corner it shows 240.00. You now know that was the amount charged to your account. Now, before you run to the bank and give them a piece of your mind, look on the back of your check to see what bank the check was deposited in as that was the bank where the error occurred; that bank will then credit your bank and your account, and you do not go to that bank, but rather to your bank.

The bank will take care of the necessary corrections. An example: let's say that you bank at bank X and you purchased some clothes from Jackie's clothing store and Jackie makes a deposit at bank Z, and it is Jackie's bank that encodes the wrong figure. This figure will go through the banking system with that figure until you notice it in your statement. Due to the fact that thousands of checks are being processed daily, it would be extremely rare that your bank would catch this mistake. Again, the point we are making here is to take care of your checking account in the correct way as that is one of the tools that will help you establish credit.

What Bankers Want To See

The question of what do bankers want to see is relatively simple because banks want deposits and the more checking account deposits, the better. This makes sense because checking account deposits, known as demand accounts, are the cheapest accounts for the banks. These accounts help you when you are applying for a loan. Banks take into consideration your account relationship when they quote you an interest rate on a loan, and the larger your average checking account balance, the better your loan interest rate should be.

Likewise, we understand how it is nice to have an account at a thrift institution because you do receive a higher rate of interest on your money, but when and if you ever need a bank loan, you will also end up paying a higher interest rate to borrow money for whatever loan amount you require. If you use a figure of twenty percent free compensating balances, you can figure on a lower interest rate. What we are talking about here is, let's say that you have an average checking balance of $2500.00 and are requesting a loan of $15,000.00, you might get one or two percent off on the interest rate because of your balance relationship with the bank. This then is important for customers who are requesting or need larger loan amounts as you will receive more consideration for any savings accounts you have at the bank. In other words, due to the cost of funds factor your interest rate break will not be as great, but it could outweigh any differences you would get by having your monies in a thrift institution. Just remember that a compensating balance is the amount of money you have on deposit at your bank and the amount of your outstanding loans.

We know of some customers who would tell us, "well, we purchased Treasury Bills through this bank," but outside of a small fee to cover the paper work the benefits of a Treasury Bill goes to the United States Government and not to the bank. Also, having a safe deposit box at a bank will not get a banker to notice you for a favorable loan interest rate. Safe deposit boxes are nothing more than a convenience being offered by banks and is one of the areas of a bank that makes very little money for the bank.

Another important subject to remember is just to be yourself when you visit your banker and not to attempt to oversell yourself by overdressing or dressing up. Over the years we have seen several kinds of dress, but the ones who overdress to impress their banker do not make a very good impression. We don't mean to imply you should spend your day in curlers and that it is proper to dress that way for a loan request appointment. The same applies to people who work in a dirty work environment as it doesn't hurt to clean up a little, but just be yourself.

Years ago Joe told me about a customer who came into the bank and he looked like he just came from a farm. As Joe started to approach this person he could tell the guy was frustrated. When Joe asked the guy if he could be of some help, he said yes and thank you. As it turned out this guy just came from the bank across the street and they had asked this guy to leave because he happened to track in some mud. As it turned out, Joe opened a savings account that day for this guy in the amount of eighty-thousand dollars. So, as anyone can now see, looks can be very deceiving, so just be yourself.

The Beginning of Credit

A lot of young people hear the same old cliche, "We are sorry but you cannot purchase this furniture, car, home, or etc., because you don't have any established credit." This is a typical situation that is repeated over and over again all across the United States. However, the people being turned down has nothing to do with their character or their trust worthiness because it does take time to establish a person's credit, therefore, our advice is to give yourself time by starting while you are young. Here is an example: When you go to a bank to ask for a loan for whatever reason and you are new on your first job and even though you have a good income, you will probably be turned down for a loan. The reason banks do this is because you do not have a credit background and should the bank decide to issue you a loan, they will require that you have a co-signer. What the bank is trying to tell you here is that they do not know if you will have the ability or stability on your job to set fixed funds aside each month to pay the loan back on time. Nevertheless, time will remedy this situation.

Banks like secured loans and those secured by savings accounts in their own bank or branch make them even happier. What you need to understand is that when banks lend you money that is secured by your own account, they are required by law to charge you at least one percent over the rate they are paying you on your account. All banks are different and some will charge you two or three percentage points over the rate they are paying you, but regardless of what it is, it is a reasonable price for you to pay. There is also the fact that the banks have minimum loan fees that can be anywhere from one hundred dollars and up depending on the particular bank. When you are applying for a loan, go into your bank and request to borrow a thousand dollars and tell your banker that you want these funds deposited into a savings account against the loan you're requesting. The banker will be pleased to hear this as their degree of exposure on the loan is the interest rate factor. When the loan is approved, ask that it be set up on monthly payments for twelve months or for a period of time that your monthly income can support. Now, during the time your loan is in effect you are accomplishing two things. First of all you are proving to your banker that you can set aside the proper amount every month to pay your monthly obligations. Secondly, you are now building a savings account and as long as you reduce your loan balance the equity in your savings account grows. Once you pay off your loan in full ask the bank to notify the major credit bureaus as this will then be your first positive indication of credit on your record, which will show that you had a secured loan that was paid as agreed. However, we need to point out here that a lot of credit bureaus will not show or indicate that the loan was a savings account loan.

To further establish and extend your credit background, we would recommend that you ask your banker to loan you some money for a period of ninety days, once again, use your savings account as security for the loan. Be prepared to pay off your loan around the eighty-fifth or eighty-ninth day and never go over the ninety-day time limit. The eighty-fifth and eighty-ninth day is important because most bank computers will send you a statement of how much you still owe about two weeks before your loan is due. Likewise, the officer that loaned you the money will also receive a computer report about ten days before your loan is due and your name and credit report will be fresh in his mind. Furthermore, when you go into the bank to pay your loan off, be sure to stop by the loan officer and tell him why you are at the bank. This is important because you are letting the loan officer know that you are around even though you may know where the note department is in the bank, but let the loan officer tell you where it is. Consequently, the loan officer is getting to know you and you are letting him know that you have paid your loan off in full.

At this time you might be thinking that you do not make enough money to pay off your loan at the specified time. However, you might have a side venture that you are expecting a return on and you could indicate this expected income at the time you are making your ninety-day loan. It would be advisable to take those funds and leave them in your checking account over this period of time. We do not recommend that you add these funds to your savings account in this instance because it would not be that beneficial. Let the banker think that you used the loan for this specified business venture as it is from that venture that the source of repayment is coming from to pay off your loan obligation. By this time you should be in your twentieth month, plus or minus a few months, working with your banker during which time your checking account has been handled correctly and you have maintained at least a hundred dollar average balance with no overdraft notifications. You also have two loans with your bank and you have proven that you can generate the monies required to pay off any loans you have had with the bank. As long as your loan request is commensurate with your income level, this then becomes a very valid and important point at your bank. The next step is to approach the bank for a loan that is about half of your savings balance. Let's say that would be around five hundred dollars and again ask for a ninety-days loan, but this time, ask that the loan be unsecured. Even though this may cause some trouble, as a lot of banks don't care to have such small loans on their books for only a ninety-day period. There is also the minimum loan charge that banks require that is to be taken into consideration and the annual percentage rate on the loan may shock you. Nevertheless, the one thing for you to remember is that the minimum loan charge and the increased interest rate is allowing you the opportunity to increase your credit status with the bank. In this situation the bank may not offer you a ninety-day note in which case you can ask them if you can have a reserve line on your checking account for this period of time. If the bank agrees the reserve line will usually be a one time advance and the account will be frozen until it is paid in full.

Another way to do this is to ask the bank to issue a Visa or Master Charge account under a one time advance, and you don't even have to concern yourself that the bank even issuing you a card at this time. However, when the loan is paid you will have shown the bank and banker that you are a responsible person. During this time you have gotten to know your banker and the people they work with and you have demonstrated your abilities to satisfy your bank loan obligations thereby establishing a good credit report.

If you have established credit in only one location with only one bank and you happen to move to another area, find a bank you like and then go back to the bank you just left where you established your credit and ask the banker if they would write you a letter of reference. Note that this is very important because people tend to move around in the US a lot and are required to reestablish their credit background in a new area. On the other hand, if you are staying with the bank where you now have established credit, its time to ask for some additional credit. Ask for a Visa or Master Card or a reserve line of credit on your checking account and you can also ask for an applications for gas cards. More than likely you will be turned down on some of your applications, but make enough of them and you will receive some. If and when you use these cards, be sure to use them to make at least one small purchase and when you receive the statement, pay it immediately, then put the card away someplace where you can't use it. The reason for this is that gas credit cards can and will get used over and over again to the point that you will not be able to get out from under them and their fees, and eventually they will end up destroying your credit history.

Over the years we have assisted many young people in establishing their credit backgrounds using the same techniques mentioned above. Likewise, some of these people were able to acquire loans up to as much as ten thousand dollars unsecured by the time they were in their early twenties. Remember, establishing credit is not hard, but it will take some time.

How to Expand Your Credit

Granted it is important to establish a solid foundation in one's credit background, but it is also important to understand and to know how to expand one's credit and yet not to expand it too much by getting one's self into financial trouble. We can't begin to tell you how many times we have heard people say, "These darn credit cards make it so easy to make purchases." Well, the fact is that these people are correct and it is not very easy for people to stop using credit cards. People need to learn how to discipline themselves and not try to expand their credit too fast and, yes, we know, it is easier said than done. The banks along with the large retail markets are causing these problems because they make it easy for people to get all the credit cards they want and then the large retail market along with the credit card companies are constantly encouraging the people to use their credit cards. The purchase now and pay later philosophy has gotten out of hand in our today's society. It's okay to use your credit card for some major purchases, but sooner or later it will get away from people if they are not careful.

Add up all your fixed monthly payments including your mortgage or rent payments, car payments, and any other term payments that you have more than three months of remaining payments. Once you come up with a figure take your gross income and divide it into the total of your payments and you'll get a percentage figure. Should your figure exceed forty-five percent you need to restrict your credit purchases immediately as you are walking a fine line of getting yourself into serious financial trouble. For your information the banks use your gross income in the above explanation, but since your gross income doesn't belong to you, we use net income figures that are the real figures that you should be looking at because these figures will keep you from getting into a financial situation that you will have a hard time getting out of if you can. It has been proven over and over again that once you exceed forty-five percent of your gross income that your chances of going bankrupt increase at a very rapid rate. On the other hand, using your net income to get to the forty-five percent figure will usually stop this from becoming a reality. Example: Let's say that your gross income is $5,000.00 a month and 45% of that would be $2,250.00 you could have in monthly maximum outgoing retail payments. Now, let's use your net income, (which the author of this book has always used) using the same figures above, you get

$5,000.00 minus 25% which comes to $1,250.00 dollars that you again subtract from the $5,000.00 gross income, and your net income is now $3,750.00 minus 45% comes to $2,062.50 leaving you a margin of $187.50 or enough room to stay out of trouble providing you stop spending until you can pay down your balance.

Naturally, there are exceptions to the rules, but the largest percentage of people will find themselves in a very tight financial situation should they reach this forty-five percent figure based on their gross income. Using your net income figure at the same forty-five percent figure will let you know that you are getting close to being in financial trouble, yet far enough away that you can get out of trouble by curbing your spending habits until you can pay down the balance and then you can start again if you have more to purchase.

Joe related another story to me that involved a young couple in California who were at a seventy-five percent retail figure based on their gross income, but managed to pull things together and get out of trouble. The only reason this couple made it out of trouble was that for three years they both worked night and day to establish their own business and to eventually payoff all of their bills. They now have a very successful business and are able to relax. There is also the situation where your gross income increases and your margins left over increases, but remember from your gross income comes your Federal and State Taxes along with other deductions, which is the difference between this figure and the forty-five percent figure that you have to cloth and feed and support your family. Otherwise known as your net income. That is why the author of this book has always used the net income figure and has never gotten himself into financial trouble. In the above discussion, by using your net income figure you should never get any closer than eight

HERE to ten percentage points away from the forty-five percent figure. Furthermore, if you reach this point, one should take a very close look at their spending habits and adjust them. It is also a lot easier to adjust your spending habits than it is to expand your income. On the other hand, should you be using your gross income figure and you start approaching the forty percent figure, people need to take a very serious look at your spending habits and adjust them as you are heading for financial trouble and possible bankruptcy. People need to realize that with the high cost of housing and interest rates the banks no longer look at the old ratios of the past. In the area of real estate lending we used to look at principal, interest, taxes, and insurance that were not to exceed twenty-five percent of your monthly income. There was also a rule we followed that indicated that we use two and a half times your yearly income, which was the maximum home a person could afford at that time. Nevertheless, with the rapid increase in the housing market over the last few decades our lending ratios increased to a standard of 28/36 percent (read as 28 over 36 in the loan industry) indicating more leeway for homebuyers. However, as home pricing continued to increase lenders would go as high as 33/45 percent providing the borrower had a good credit background.

What this all means is that we are now going be using more of our net income to cover the basic cost of housing. This is what people have been doing in other countries for decades. Moreover, this leaves us with a lesser percentage between our housing cost and the limit to which we can expand our credit. It also indicates that in the future more and more people will get into severe financial difficulties because they will be expanding their credit way too fast. We have also heard people indicate that it is cheaper to purchase an item now as it will be paid back in cheaper dollars. This may be true to a certain point, but by purchasing this item today, one is pushed over the forty-five percent bracket, then the people should be prepared for some serious financial problems. Granted it might be cheaper to purchase the item today, but wait until you have the cash to pay for the item.

Small Business Credit

If a small or medium size business decides to approach a bank for a loan request it is important that they do it in an appropriate way. There have been several times that loan applications have been submitted to banks and once a loan officer analyzes the information, he states, "Who are they trying to fool?" It's not like the loan officer is turning you down or indicating that your business loan request is not needed. They are simply looking at the facts as presented in your application and the facts do not add up. There are several small things you can do to make sure your facts are being presented in the correct way. Usually, small businesses will try to do their own bookkeeping or hire a service so you can see exactly where you are at the end of each month. Once you have reached a certain business volume you will usually expand to a public accountant and then to a certified public accountant. When you receive your financial statement, make sure you understand everything in the statement. There is one thing here that we will point out, which is that your tax returns for the business agree with your business statement. If it does not agree, then an explanation needs to be indicated in the footnotes. In the event a business is a corporation there will be an area in your tax returns where you can adjust the business statement to your tax return. However, a business statement is rather self-explanatory when prepared by a certified public account. It is important to know that your personal financial statement be filled out with real figures that can be verified.

As far as stock is concerned there is a place in your statement to list your unlisted stock, but be careful as time and time again we have noticed some very distorted figures in this location. Okay, your financial statement on your business has your business showing a net worth of $75,000.00 and where it indicates your stock, assuming you own one hundred percent of your business stock be sure to put the $75,000.00 in this area. As funny as it may seem, we have seen figures in excess of a half a million dollars to be used as the stock value and when it is compared with your business financial statement, we usually see figures 10 to 15 times smaller. We also realize that you could indicate your business is worth more than its net worth, but if you want to inflate the net worth, you need to use a figure that you can support. We have also seen businesses with net worths of a quarter of a million dollars that had offers over a million dollars from qualified buyers. Should you have something like this occur, then you can justify increasing the figure. Just make sure your financial statement makes sense and your figures can be supported. Another major area that gets blown out of proportion on a statement is real estate, and again it is important to use realistic values on real estate. Showing you purchased a home five months ago for $200,000,00 and now it's worth $250,000.00, you need to be able to justify the increase in value of your real estate. Granted there may be an explanation to the increased value of your property, but you need to be ready to explain and justify the reason for the increased value. Like we said before there are always exceptions to the rule and in this situation we had a customer's statement who indicated an initial land purchase for $50,000.00 dollars that she bought in March of a given year and in September of that same year she indicated the land was worth a little over three million dollars. Even the weakest of bankers would question and challenge this situation. As it turned out this customer was completely prepared and what she stated was all true. She had entered into an agreement several years prior from an estate and the estate agreed to sell her this land and her money was placed into an escrow account. It took several years for the estate to close and in March of that year she received fee titled to the land. There were several reasons for the delay of the estate and one of the reasons occurred about three years into the purchase of this land. As it turned out someone decided that this land would be the perfect site for a major baseball stadium. As it turned out the estate liked that idea and it took the buyer four years in court before she was finally authorized to go ahead with the purchase of the land as agreed in the contract for $50,000.00 dollars. In this situation it indicates that the land buyer knew she would probably have to answer questions concerning the land value and she saved a considerable amount of trouble having the land put into an escrow account as she had the answers when the time came.

Another area in your statement that you will need to justify is your personal property. This figure will comprise everything that was not included in your previous statement. Also, when it comes to silver, gold, diamonds, major furniture, and artworks that can constantly go up and down in value, be sure to list those values separately. Make sure you have these items appraised and you just might be surprised at the value these items will have. There is also a place on the financial statement to indicate your yearly income and be sure to indicate whether the income is taxable or not. This is another area where people will inflate their income as opposed to what they actually receive. A banker will request your last year's tax returns that should agree with what you state on your financial statement. In the event that these figures do not agree, then you need to be able to explain to the banker where you derived your income.

We have seen situations where the financial statement shows a $130,000.00 dollars in income and the tax returns show $30,000.00 dollars in adjusted gross income. Even though this may be correct, be sure to take your whole tax return to the bank so they can go back through your returns in order to justify your figures. This is very essential because you may have a lot of depreciation and your real cash flow may be a lot better then you have lead the banker to believe. On an on-going basis you should always continue to analyze and know your banking situation so that you can plan ahead for your business needs and requirements. Bankers don't like it when someone comes in and tells them that they needed the money yesterday. Even though this may sound strange, this situation happens all too often and unless you have established a strong relationship with your bank, you might just find yourself out in the street.

Learn and Know Your Bank's Limits

A bank's limitations are found in two areas, one being the services they offer and the other is how the lending structure works. It is imperative that you know in what areas in the lending field a bank places their emphasis on because you may be banking at the wrong bank for your business needs. Also, all banks advertise that they are full service banks because they offer many diversified services. However, even though this may be true, they may specialize in only a particular type of loan over others. There are certain banks that offer SBA loans, (Small Business Administration), but they will inform you right away that they do not make this type of loan. Other banks will stress that they make interim-construction loans, but not accounts receivables. Others will specialize in floating lines of credit and other banks do not care to make long term real-estate loans, yet they are very active in the home equity and home improvement loan areas.

This is why we stress that it is imperative that you understand the lending limits of your particular bank. If you are doing business with a bank that has a legal lending limit of two hundred and fifty-thousand dollars and you need five hundred thousand dollars or more in accounts receivables line of credit, then you need to evaluate your bank's situation, especially, if you plan to grow and be successful in your business. Granted the smaller bank will be able to do a five hundred thousand dollar account receivables credit line, but they will be working with other small banks or its major correspondent bank who shares in the loan. On the other hand, if you are dealing with larger banks, then it may not make any difference to you or your business. When selecting your bank, take a good hard look at your business and try to project and evaluate whether or not your business banking needs can be met by your bank in future years. The majority of people are already with proper banks, but there may be a few who need to analyze their expanding banking credit needs.

We often hear people tell us that they have been turned down by a bank's loan committee, which we find to be a very interesting statement as most of the time it is not a loan committee who turned your loan down, but rather it was the banker or his supervisor of the loan department who said no. The primary reason for this diversion tactic is that it makes it a lot easier for the banker to inform you that it was the bank's loan committee that turned you down as people are not inclined to question that decision. On larger loans or credit requests it just may be a loan committee who turns you down, but on loans or credit request under $50,000.00 dollars, the person you were looking at and talking with turned you down or the person they report to for loan approval turned you down.

It is necessary to understand your bank's loan limits and how they work because the loan limit is the maximum amount established by a bank that their loan officers are able to lend to any one customer. The loan limit would also include all of the debt a customer would have with their bank. Let's say the branch manager had a loan limit of $30,000.00 dollars and your current loan debt with the bank is $15,000.00 dollars and you would like a loan to buy a vehicle for $25,000.00 dollars. Remember, the bank manager will know what kind of loans the bank wants along with the credit requirements they will expect. When the bank manager glances at your loan request and notices that it will not conform to the bank's requirements, he/she could technically turn you down right then. However, most of the time this will not happen even though the bank will not authorize the loan. Because the chances of you getting a loan are not good, he/she will tell you that they will get back to you in a couple of days. There are situations where the manager will not even present your loan request up the corporate ladder because they know their loan supervisor might question their abilities concerning the understanding of the bank's loan guidelines. Normally, you will get a call or a letter in a couple of days that will explain the reason why the bank's loan committee turned your loan request down. It is also highly unlikely that the bank will inform you that his/her supervisor turned you down or that there is no bank loan committee and that they did nothing with your loan application but run a credit report. The real fact of the matter is that you exceeded the bank's loan limit because the bank's loan limit was $30,000.00 dollars and with your current loan of $15,000.00 dollars and your new loan request for $25,000.00 dollars would take you to $40,000.00 dollars, which would be $10,000.00 dollars over the bank's loan limit.

It, therefore, is crucial that you comprehend how the banking system functions so that you can submit your credit request with the knowledge of how the banks work. Like the situation mentioned above, once the bank manager gives his approval on the loan, the credit manager becomes responsible to his/her loan supervisor. The loan supervisor will only see you on paper and it is unlikely that you will ever meet this mystery person. One of the essential circumstances of a loan credit decision is the disposition of the person with whom we are dealing with that will never be revealed or show up on any paperwork, but as a bank manager we need to include this in our presentations. In the event that you have been turned down by your bank for a loan request, be sure to ask why you believe that the explanation being given is incorrect, and make sure that you elucidate that to your loan officer. There have been several loans at banks all across the United States where the persons requesting a loan were turned down and because of their strong will, these people were able to have their banker/loan officer change their minds.

There are several banks that have many different ways of establishing their lending authority, and we know of a couple of banks in California where the managers have the authority to manage about ninety percent of all their bank's loan requests. Smaller banks may make larger loan commitments and all banks have loan committees that are not usually used as much as people are led to believe. Some banks allow loan officers to merge their loan limits. In this circumstance you have two loan officers that each have a loan authority of $50,000.00 dollars and once merged they can make a loan of $100,000.00 dollars. There are additional banks that will let their loan officers loan up to half the bank's legal lending limit. Again it is vital that you learn that every bank is different in the area of substantiating loan authority. Usually, the branch or the bank manager will have the largest loan limit in the bank. Normally, in the independent banking system the senior loan officer or the president of the bank will have this lending authority. Correspondingly, there are extremely large banks that maintain large branch offices where the bank managers may have loan authority of up to a half a million dollars. That is why it is extremely necessary that you have the understanding of who you're dealing with and determine if that person is the correct person that can handle these kinds of loans that you may need now or in the future to come.

It Can be Worth it to Shop Around

Is it likely for a small investor to survive it in today's world of high interest? The answer is a definite yes, but they need to be more aware of what is going on in the world of finance. People cannot expect to save a major percentage of their paycheck like they have in the past. Therefore, you have to ask yourself, when do you save it when inflation is on the rise? Likewise, when people are in need of a loan, they should shop around as you should do with everything else people would like, want, or need. It would also be smart to make several calls because you just might be amazed at the amount of savings you could get just talking to different people you're contemplating doing business with. All banks have interest rates, but different banks have different interest rates for different kinds of loans. Save yourself some money by simply calling different banks and asking what they would charge in interest rates for the type of loan you are interested in applying for. Also, don't forget to call your bank where you maintain your bank accounts as this will give you some leverage. Should you own your own business and maintain your business account at a different bank than your personal account, be sure to call that bank also.

Allow me to reiterate another story Joe related to me years ago. Joe knew of a businessman that was successful who he knew through an associate that wanted another car loan. Apparently, this person told Joe that he had gone to his bank where he had three previous vehicle loans and was quoted an interest rate of 19% simple interest. When Joe asked him if this was the same bank that he had his personal accounts at, this businessman said no. Joe then told him to call his bank and ask them what they could do concerning a car loan for him. Several weeks later the businessman called Joe back to inform him that he had gotten a five percent discount off the interest rate the other bank quoted him. Now, this may not sound like much, but for a new car financed for five years the interest rate savings would be considerable. Granted that the story we just related to you may not be a situation that you might get yourself into, but it happens over and over every day across America. However, the point being made is that if you take the time required to shop around, you can save yourself considerable money in financing.

When you are calling around for rates, be sure to ask if the loan will be simple interest or add-on interest. Simple interest installment loans will operate similar to a mortgage loan on your home and if you make a payment that is larger than your regular house payment, the difference will be applied to the principal that will reduce the principal balance of your home loan.

Furthermore, if the bank does not offer a simple interest installment loan program they will be offering an add-on interest rate loan. This type of loan is where a bank figures the interest rate charges for the period of time of the loan and adds that to the principal amount borrowed and then divides that figure by the number of months you are requesting for your installment loan. Also, with the add-on interest loan, the bank will earn most of the interest charged back in the first part of the loan term. Therefore, if you decide to pay the loan off early, the amount of interest that you will get back will be less. On the other hand, with a simple interest rate installment loan, you will save yourself some interest back on the loan should you decide to pay off the loan prior to the loan's maturity date.

If or when one ever decides to get a home improvement loan, call your bank and the other banks located in your area and check to see what interest rates are along with the cost of the loan in points. Be sure to ask the bank if there will be any prepayment charges in the event you pay the loan off early. Note that several dealers also offer home improvement loans as they probably have made arrangements with different financial institutions, but their interest rates are usually higher than the interest rates the banks may be offering. Remember, that banks have several different and alternative loan programs all having variable service charges with the accounts, so be sure to check around your area to get the best interest rates being offered as you can save yourself a considerable amount of money. But, be aware that most banks who are offering overdraft lines of credit on a checking account will usually waive any service charges. Again, the banks can only charge you when you use your line of credit.

Most banks will charge you for checks, but it is reasonable even though the banks make a small profit. Banks do lose money on safe deposit box rentals, but they cannot afford to lose in other areas or they would go out of business. However, you should ask the bank what the minimum amount is required in a checking or savings account to wave all check fees and other bank charges. Again, all banks will have different fees in order to get free bank services on everything including free cashier or traveler checks. Some banks may require a minimum balance of five thousand, ten thousand, or as much as fifteen thousand dollars that must be maintained monthly in an account in order for people to be granted these free services. Again it doesn't make any difference what accounts these amounts are in as long as one meets the bank's minimum requirements. On savings accounts that are over one hundred thousand dollars, it pays to shop different banks as you may gain as much as one and a half or two percent more interest on your money. As we stated before it pays to shop around and this is true for any type of loan and be sure to call or stop by your bank when you are first starting out.

Things to Remember About Banks and Banking

The information we have put forth in this bonus section will give anyone the tools and skills to start your credit and establish your credit background and eventually increase your credit in the future to meet or satisfy your needs. We have seen several different statistics that indicated that if a person only looked, they would have found what they were looking for in their own backyard. Look at your bank first and then begin looking at other banks, and if you don't like what you're hearing, or your bank doesn't offer you what you're looking for in the way of services try another bank. As a rule, banks will offer their customers most of the financial services that they will need and usually, at a lower rate than if you used the services of another bank, but this may or may not be the case in your situation so shop around.

It is imperative that you get to know the appropriate people in the bank where you're doing business. It is also essential to remember that bankers have egos and you need to play on their egos. We also want to point out to people that bankers usually have more knowledge on the subject matter you maybe discussing, but use general psychology and play on the banker's ego. Remember, introduce yourself in a positive way and let them know that you are or will be one of their customers. There maybe a circumstance that comes up where your first introduction to a bank officer is due to a negative situation. In the event that this happens do not enter the bank with an attitude of I got you now, but rather show some consideration and turn the negative situation into a positive introduction. In this situation, the fact that you're showing self-restraint may save you several dollars at a later date when you may need some sort of credit.

The best way to begin your credit future is to maintain your checking account in the appropriate way and try to maintain a balance of at least a hundred dollars or more in your account at all times. Be careful that you do not write a check before you make a deposit and be certain to make sure the deposit is in the hands of the teller and recorded in the bank's computer. There are a massive amount of people today who bank with their computers online, but just because you use this method of banking, don't think that it is okay to start writing checks. Until your bank clears the deposit and it has been recorded into the bank's computer, you technically do not have a valid deposit.

Although some people get by with writing checks, they are basically counting on the float factor and they do not realize it or what they are doing. Unless you have a hundred percent confidence and trust that your bank has recorded your deposit in the bank's computer, just hold off for a day. Furthermore, you do not want to write a check before your bank's cutoff time for that day.

We have also discussed the information that is retained in the computer when your account is overdrawn. The computer also maintains information on any loans that you may have at the bank. Nonetheless, even though most people believe that they have ten days or so to make their payment or payments, they are considered past due by the bank's computer and the majority of the people believe they have thirty days before they are considered late or have a problem where they are banking. Normally, the bank's computer will not report you having a late payment on a loan until five days after the payment is past due assuming your loan was due on the first of the month. The next computer print out will be on the tenth of the month, and believe us, this is the one you do not want to have showing up on the computer readout. You may be asking yourself why this is so important and it is because banks will report this to the credit reporting agencies on how many ten-day late notices you have had and this will be reflected as derogatory credit on your credit report. Should your loan payment due date not correspond with your pay period or your pay period has been changed, go to your bank and ask them to change the due date on your loan or loans.

All the above information is critical because you definitely don't want any ten-day late notices showing up on your credit report. There may be times that you have told your loan officer that you will be late with a loan payment thinking that it will be okay and the loan officer responds saying that it will be okay. Granted, the loan officer will mark a reporting sheet in front of you. Then at the loan officers meeting they will make their reports, but what they don't tell you is that they do not change the bank's computer memory, and sitting in the bank's computer is the ten-day late reported on your record. So, when your loan is paid in full and reported to the credit agencies, someone in their backroom who has never seen your file will pull your information from the computer and report only that which the computer has stored in it. The point being made is to make your payments on time or ask the bank to change your due date. Also, make sure and ask that they can have the computer not indicate the late payment.

When you are establishing credit, make sure your introduction is positive, and yes, we know that we are being repetitive, but it is essential that you make a good rememberable impression with the right people. Since there are several thousands of banks all across the US, you can be selective even though the majority of people look for a bank out of convenience. Even though you may have to go a little out of your way, the rewards you will receive can be more than worth it. In reference to venture capital loans, note that banks do not generally care for making or granting these loans. The reason for this is because the bank is putting up most or all of the up-front money for you to set yourself up in business. So, if your loan request is for venture capital, be ready to have some collateral for the bank. Normally, a bank will ask for some kind of security other than something like inventory, equipment, or contracts related to your business. It might be a good idea to meet with a business financial consultant to look over your business plan before approaching a bank. Should you not care to pay a financial consultants fee, then lay out your business plan in advance and then take it to a banker and ask for their advice. Be sure to start slowly so as not to indicate that you are there for a large business loan. Likewise, play on the ego of the banker and use the right psychology when you want to make your loan request later on in the discussion. Make sure your business loan is realistic and ask for more than you really need. Let's say you need $25,000.00 dollars, ask for $30,000.00 and let the banker back the loan request down to $25,000.00 and yes, bankers will do this, but you will still have the funding you originally needed.

Banks are in business just like any other business, so be sure to shop around to find a bank that meets your needs. Think about banks like you would shopping for a car, furniture, or appliances because you're basically doing the same thing when shopping for a loan. The money that you save can be a large return for a few hours of work on the phone or by making personal contacts. People seeking larger loans may think that their time is too valuable to shop for loans, but the cost in points alone can be as much as five or six points between different banks. On a loan of a $150,000.00 dollars, this can equate to $9,000.00 dollars saved and on a $250,000.00 dollar loan, one could save as much as $15,000.00 dollars just in points alone for a few hours of work. If, on the other hand, you are making five-hundred or a thousand dollars an hour, you can afford to let someone else do the work for you.

WISHING YOU GOOD LUCK AND HAPPY

SHOPPING